TRADITIONS

OF THE

NAVY

TRADITIONS
OF THE
NAVY

by Cedric W. Windas

Edited by

LCDR Arnold S. Lott, USN(Ret)

Published by

LEEWARD PUBLICATIONS, INC.
Annapolis, Maryland

Library of Congress Catalog Card No. 78-699-43

ISBN No. 0-915268-15-9

Design by Andrea Pratt

Back cover rendering by Alan B. Chesley

Printed by The John D. Lucas Company
Baltimore, Maryland

This book is for arm-chair navigators, dock watchers, rail birds, old shellbacks, young swabs, deep sea sailors, beachcombers, and all those who like the flavor of salt in their reading.

Preface

Every ship that puts to sea, whether she be a cod fisherman bound for the Grand Banks, an aircraft carrier being "chopped" to the 7th Fleet, or a jumbo tanker headed for the Cape and the Gulf of Bahrein, carries a full allowance of rule books and regulations. Routine at sea these days must "go by the book." Yet every one of those ships also carries her share of seagoing tradition, custom—even superstition, if you will—that may not be quoted in the books yet is as much a part of life at sea now as it was when Ulysses cruised the Aegean Sea and the Phoenicians sailed down to Egyptland, over two thousand years ago.

What sailor—or master—would want to sail in a ship that had not been properly christened? Yet christening is a heathen custom dating back to at least 2100 B.C. One salutes the quarter deck when boarding a naval vessel—but so did men boarding their ships in the days of Greek, Roman, and Carthaginian sea power. Practically all naval vessels, and many others—even yachts—have coins placed under the step of the mast. There's no regulation about this, but tradition, now several thousand years old, decrees the custom. It began long before the rule books were written, when Romans placed coins in the mouths of the dead so they could pay Charon for transporting them across the river Styx. "It's just a superstition," say the cynics—but after all, it costs only a few coins, so why take a chance?

The tradition of the sea know no national boundaries, and they are observed by seagoing men, whether they wear the uniform of a naval service, the merchant marine, the fishing fleet, or the serious yachtsmen. No matter who or what they may be, when they leave the land astern, they are all at sea—on the same sea sailed by Magellan, Columbus, Drake, John Paul Jones and Joshua Slocum.

But one need not go to sea in order to discover the colorful customs, the exotic langauge, and the sometimes archaic terminology that sets sailors apart from landsmen. Here have been collected a luckybag full of traditions, customs, slang, odd facts, and other miscellaneous bits of information that have only one aspect in common; they are all slightly soaked in salt water. Perusal of this book will not result in promotion to "ruler of the Queen's Na-vee," nor even qualification as skipper of a shrimp boat out of Key Largo, but it will furnish some understanding of why those who follow the sea feel a brotherhood with the seamen of all nations.

As many of the U.S. Navy's traditions originated in that much older service, the Royal Navy, it is fitting to repeat here a few words by an Englishman—and a sailor—Joseph Conrad: "The mysteriously born tradition of sea craft commands unity in an occupation in which men have to depend on each other." Finally, the sea itself commands unity of understanding among those who sail on it, write about it, or merely read about it—no one can deny ". . . the beauty and mystery of the ships, and the magic of the sea." *

Arnold S. Lott

---

* Henry Wadsworth Longfellow, "My Lost Youth."

Cedric W. Windas was born in Richmond, Victoria, Australia, on 4 March 1888. After completing his education in the public schools of Melbourne, he went to sea as an apprentice in the steel-hulled, full-rigged ship *Segura;* he eventually became second mate of the inter-island trading schooner *Amy Moir.* Both ships sailed under the British flag.

After his marriage, Windas entered the field of commercial art and advertising, first in Melbourne, and then in Honolulu, Hawaii, where he became a feature writer and cartoonist for the Honolulu *Morning Advertsiser.* Then he moved to Los Angeles, where he spent four years as feature writer and cartoonist for the old Los Angeles *Evening Express,* which later became the *Herald Examiner.*

Subsequently Windas became a free lance writer, contributing articles to some 35 national magazines, including *Argosy, Adventure,* and *Power Boating.* He also produced many magazine covers, and gained wide recognition for his paintings of sailing vessels.

The art work and text of this book was produced about 1930, and first appeared as a monthly feature in *Our Navy* Magazine for over a decade. The book was published in 1942, but has been out of print for many years. This revised, up-dated edition has been made possible through the cooperation and interest of his son, Captain Jack M. Windas of the American President Lines, and a long-time friend, Gladys Stewart of Hermosa Beach, California.

Cedric Windas died on 4 December 1966. A most unusual monument to his memory may be seen in the Cabrillo Beach Marine Museum, San Pedro, California. It is a scale model of a brig named *Tradition,* pictured here with Cedric Windas, who spent seven years building it. Valued at $35,000, it is the largest such model in the world—12'6" long and 14'1" from keel to truck. A photograph of the model under sail appears in the back of the book.

Continental Navy, the forerunner of the United States Navy, was established on 13 October 1775. The first four ships in the Navy were all named for foreigners: *Alfred* (for King Alfred the Great who founded the British Navy between 878–900 AD); *Columbus* (for Christopher Columbus who discovered the New World in 1492); *Cabot* (for John Cabot, who was really an Italian named Giovanni Caboto, the first English explorer of America); and *Andrew Doria* (for Andrea Doria, a Genoese admiral who lived at the same time as Columbus).

Sword salute • The first movement of a modern sword salute is a survival of the ancient custom of kissing the cross which was emblazoned on the hilt of every sword carried by a Christian.

The Old, Old Navy • King Minos of Crete is said to have established the first regularly organized Navy, which he did about 1400 BC.

Salute the quarter deck. This custom comes from the days when Roman warships carried pagan shrines, and obeisances to these shrines were made to appease the gods of the sea. Later, the same respect was paid to the shrine of the Virgin. The quarter deck is saluted, whether or not the flag is flying.

"*Shanghai,*" meaning to send a man aboard ship against his will by using force, drugs or liquor, comes down from sailing-ship days when it was difficult to get full crews and shipmasters would pay shady characters on the beach to hustle unconscious sailors aboard their ships. Many men were thus shipped to Shanghai, or other ports; some were probably shipped out of Shanghai in the same way.

"*Cumshaw*" is Navy slang meaning "a little extra on the side," or "something for nothing." It comes from the Chinese *kam sia* used by beggers to express "grateful thanks."

Maskee • Pidgin English for *very good.*
Dinghow • Oriental, for *very good.*

"*Can do*" is pidgin English for assent or agreement. Disagreement is *no can do.*

"*Gung ho*" from the Chinese, meaning to have an eager and determined attitude; a real eager beaver.

Fire chiefs is a nickname used aboard vessels in the Orient for coolies who "ran amuck." They are known as "fire chiefs" because they invariably grab up a fire-axe before sallying forth to wreak vengeance on the ship's company.

Tattoos, first worn by natives in various Pacific Islands, were later adopted by illiterate seamen as a means of identification. At one time tattoos were the "in" thing for the most elite members of society. Tattoos are again a means of identification; some people have their Social Security numbers tattooed on a handy spot, and pet owners discourage "dognappers" by having their dogs tattooed.

2

Dog House • This is a perfectly good nautical term, referring to a small box-like cabin on a modern yacht. But slang usage, "in the dog house," means to be in disfavor or disgrace, and it originated in the early 1800s, during the slave trade. Slave ships filled every nook and cranny with their unfortunate cargo, and sometimes put slaves in the officer's cabins. The officers then slept on deck in small box-like structures which were nicknamed "dog houses." They were most uncomfortable, so the term "in the dog house" originated to describe being in a tough spot.

Sick bays aboard ship were originally called "sick berths." As they were generally located in the rounded stern, the contour of the space suggested a bay, and that name later replaced berth.

Room to swing a cat • This phrase, was coined in an era when it was often customary to flog men in the ship's brig. If the brig was too small to allow full play for the cat-o'-nine-tails, the culprit would be taken on deck and there punished for his misdeeds.

"Round-bottomed chest" was old Navy slang for a sailor's carry-all, his sea bag.

Poop deck, the after deck of a ship, receives its name from the old Roman custom of carrying *pupi* (small images of their gods) in the stern of their ships for luck.

Brig, meaning two-masted square-rigged ship was derived from the word *brigandine,* a name for pirates or outlaws in the Levant—the eastern part of the Mediterranean. Brig, meaning the compartment aboard ship in which prisoners are confined, comes from the fact that Admiral Nelson once used such a ship to confine prisoners taken during a naval engagement. Now, any jail can be a brig.

3

Starboard—the right side of a ship. Because the Vikings shipped their *star*, or steering oar, on the right hand side of their vessels, and called the side of a ship its *board*, the right hand side of ships has, ever since, been called the star-board side.

Lateen sails, mainsails cut to a triangular shape, were originally called *latin* sails, in order to designate the rig of Mediterranean-type vessels.

Taffrail is a rail at the stern of a vessel. Some experts maintain that taffrail is a combination of three words, namely: the after rail. Others claim it is a misspelling of the Dutch word *tafareel* which meant painting on the stern.

Fife rail • The pin rail at the base of a mast was named for the little fife-and-drum boys who perched there out of the way while men-o'-warsmen manuevered or drilled to the shrill note of the fife and drum tattoo. Fife and drum have long since disappeared, but the rail still retains it's old name.

Larboard side was the old-time name for the modern "port" or left-hand side of a vessel; it meant literally "loading" side. The first ships were steered by a huge oar secured near the stern, on the starboard or right-hand side. In order to keep the steering oar from being crushed against the side of the dock, ships always tied up left-side fast to the wharf, and the left-hand side was called the "lar" or "load"-board side.

4

Forecastle, pronounced *focsul,* is the forward main deck of a ship and, in sailing ships, the crew's quarters. In antiquity, ships had large raised platforms, resembling wooden castles, built at bow and stern, from which spears, arrows and even fire bombs were thrown on an enemy.

Ammunition, referring to powder and projectiles, comes from the French *munire,* meaning "to provide."

Unsinkable Island • The little 9-mile long island of Kahoolawe, about 90 miles from Hawaii, was the most shot-at piece of land in all of World War II. Between 1943 and 1947, more than 800 ships used it as a target for bombing and gunnery practice.

Acey-Ducey • Seagoing version of backgammon.

Firing a bale of hay • Said of a gunnery error in which a powder charge is fired without a projectile in the gun—lots of noise but no damage to the target.

Hand grenades. These deadly little weapons were probably invented by Chinese pirates, who packed gunpowder into short lengths of bamboo and fitted each one with a fuze much like a firecracker.

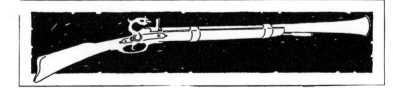

Blunderbuss, a clumsy firearm with a trumpet-shaped muzzle, gets its name from the old Dutch *donder-bus* (thunder-gun). The *buss* probably is a corruption of "Bess," after the English weapon of the same time, called "Brown Bess."

Taps, the bugle call marking the end of the daily routine aboard ship or at a military post, comes from the Dutch *taptoe,* or time to close up the taps (spigots) in taverns and bars. Tattoo, the call sounded just before taps, comes from the same source word. The notes for taps as sounded in the U.S. were composed by General Daniel Butterfield and were first played in July 1862.

Head • Toilet, powder room, WC, john, or comfort station, as the case may be.

"Pale ale" was old Navy slang for a plain drink of water from the scuttlebutt.

"Sundowner," in the old Navy, was a nickname for an officer who insisted that all hands to be aboard the ship at sundown.

Gangway, the narrow platform by which one boards or leaves a ship, received its name from the plank or platform which extended from stem to stern on slave-galleys, where the whip-master used a lash to encourage the oarsmen.

Swabbo! • You missed it!

Foxtail • A counter brush.

"Irish hurricane" is slang for a dead calm.

Spud coxswain • A man who prepares vegetables for the galley.

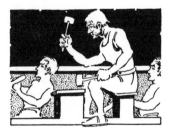

"Knock-off" is slang for quit work, or "stop whatever it is you are doing." When boats were rowed by galley slaves, a man beat time for them with a mallet and block of wood. While he kept knocking the mallet on the block, they rowed; when he stopped knocking, they could stop rowing.

"Banian days" meant "rabbit food," so far as sailors were concerned when the British navy, as a measure of economy, ruled that sailors would have two meatless days per week. Sneering sailors referred to such days as "Banian days," naming them for the Hindu Banians, a tribe whose religion prohibited any diet other than vegetarian.

George Washington was many things, but no sailor. But he tried. As a young man he was determined to go to sea, against the objections of his parents, and got as far as a waterfront saloon where men were being rounded up for a crew. The officer in charge recognized George, and he was sent home, thus setting him up to become the first president instead of, perhaps, first admiral.

First Sea-going President • Franklin D. Roosevelt was the first U.S. president to sail his own vessel to a foreign port. He took his schooner *Amberjack* to Campo Bello, Canada, on a vacation cruise.

Presidents at Sea • The President of the United States is the Commander in Chief of the Navy. But some presidents were in the Navy long before they dreamed of becoming commander in chief. In 1942, the Navy had four officers on active duty, all of whom became president, one after another. They were Lieutenant John F. Kennedy, 35th President; Lieutenant Commander Lyndon B. Johnson, 36th President; Lieutenant Commander Richard M. Nixon, 37th President; and Lieutenant Commander Gerald Ford, 38th President. The 39th President of the United States, listed in naval records as James Earl Carter, Jr., served from June 1946 until October 1953, when he resigned as a Lieutenant.

Soldiering, a slang term for loafing on the job, comes down from the times when soldiers aboard ship did their share of fighting, but refused to have anything to do with working the ship, as they felt that was beneath their dignity.

Blue Monday • This expression came into use as early as the 18th century, when it was a custom aboard ship to log a man's misdeeds daily as they were committed. The culprits were all flogged weekly, on Monday.

Bean jockey • A man who helps serve food.

Stick-in-the-mud, a term for a person who is non-progressive or of no account, had a gruesome origin. When English pirates were hanged, their bodies were buried in the mud of the Thames River so that no one might ever find them.

Coffin ships, in the maritime insurance business, refers to old un-seaworthy craft over-insured by their owners and sent to sea with the idea of deliberately sinking them.

Blasphemy can hurt. Blasphemy, and obscene and profane language, is not the mark of a true sailorman. In Queen Elizabeth's reign, blasphemy was punished by burning the offender's tongue with a hot iron.

Paint washers, in the language of the old hairy-chested sea-dogs of square-rigger days, were the young upstarts who served aboard the new-fangled steamships, where there were no lines or sails to handle—nothing to do but wash paint.

Two of a kind • The USS *Shaw,* operating off the British Isles in World War I, collided with another ship and lost her bow. He skipper turned her around and sailed her to port backwards, where another bow was fitted. The second ship named *Shaw* was wrecked during the Japanese attack on Pearl Harbor, 7 December 1941—her bow was blown off. A temporary bow was fitted, she sailed back to the United States for rebuilding, and fought successfully all through World War II.

Marine swords • Swords worn by present-day Marine officers are almost exact duplicates of one presented to William Eaton by the Bey of Tripoli during the war with the Barbary Powers back in 1804–05. Eaton helped lead a band of Marines, sailors, and tribesmen on camels across the desert from Alexandria to Tripoli, in North Africa. It was that expedition which gave the Marines the phrase "to the shores of Tripoli" in the Marines' Hymn.

Ships by the hundreds • Merchant ships sometimes sail in convoys during wartime, but in peacetime they usually operate singly and congregated only in port. Contrary to what one might expect, the greatest assemblies of ships were not always in the big ports of the world. Perhaps an all-time record for ships in one place was set in the 1840s, when as many as 400 ships would be anchored at one time, off the African island of Ichaboe, where they waited to load guano. A few years later there were even more ships in the harbor at San Francisco, but these were *abandoned.* In the rush to get to the newly discovered gold fields, entire crews deserted their ships, and in July 1849 there were 526 ships without captain or crew; many others had been sunk or beached.

Scratch the cat • After a couple of centuries of faithful service, Britain's seagoing pussycats are out of work. The cats began going to sea in 18th-century wooden ships, to combat the huge rats that infested them. Modern container ships have largely eliminated the rat problem. Fear that cats might bring rabies into Britain from overseas has led to the order to keep cats off ships. So, after March 1977, British ships no longer carried cats—they were all put ashore.

Ships named for a family • Three ships in the U.S. Navy have each been named for several members of the same family. The *O'Brien* was named for five brothers who served during the Revolutionary War; the *Ellet* was named for five members of the Ellet family; and the *Nicholson* was named for five members of that family. *The Sullivans* was named for five brothers, killed at Guadalcanal. Several ships, *John Rodgers, Hollister, Rogers, Gearing,* and *Barber,* were named for three members of the same family.

Ship with a plural name • The destroyer, *The Sullivans,* was named in honor of five brothers of the Sullivan family who were lost when the USS *Juneau* was sunk off Guadalcanal on 15 November 1942. George Thomas, Francis Henry, Joseph Eugene, Madison Abel and Albert Leo Sullivan had all enlisted at Waterloo, Iowa, on 3 January 1942.

Homeward bound pennant is a flag flown by a ship returning to the United States after she has been overseas for nine months or more. It flies from the time she starts home until sunset of her first day in a U.S. port. Next to the hoist, the flag carries a star for the first nine months overseas, and additional stars for each six months. It is one foot long for each man on board, but never longer than the length of the ship. Frequently balloons are used to keep a long pennant from dragging in the water. After the pennant is taken down, it is cut up and a piece goes to every person on board the ship.

Touching the stars • This sentimental custom started when Annapolis midshipmen were making training cruises to Europe. French and Scandinavian girls would touch the stars on the midshipman's dress uniforms, in the hope that it would bring them (the girls) good luck.

Nowadays the underlying thought has undergone a change. When a woman (wife, mother, sister or sweetheart) is bidding farewell to her departing sailor, she touches the stars on his uniform as a silent wish for his safe keeping and happy return.

Blue moon is a rare celestial event, so the expression "Once in a blue moon" means "very rarely indeed." Under certain atmospheric conditions the moon *does* appear to have a blue tinge to it. The "green flash" of the sun is much more common. At sea, on a clear evening, refraction of light in the atmosphere will produce a brilliant green flash just as the upper arc of the sun drops below the horizon.

"Feeling blue," or having a fit of the blues, means one feels melancholy, rotten, or perhaps "lousy." It used to be a custom, among deepwater sailors, when the ship lost a captain or officer during a voyage, to fly blue flags and paint a blue band along the ship's hull when entering port.

Halfmasting Colors • During the ceremony of burial at sea, the ensign is flown at halfmast. On shore stations, the ensign is also flown at halfmast during the ceremony and sometimes for a period before and after, depending on the rank of the deceased. On the death of a person of national importance, such as the president, the flag may be flown at halfmast for a period of several days.

Painting of naval vessels • Ships have been painted almost every color there is; battleship gray is only one of them. Black was standard until 1888, when the Navy changed to white to reduce heat in ships in tropical waters. White lasted until 1908, when grey became standard except for when camouflage was required. During World War II ships wore mixtures of gray, black, white, green and blue.

Red Duster, the nickname for the flag flown by ships in the British Merchant Navy. It is properly called the Red Ensign. It originated during the reign of Queen Anne (1702–1714), when it was called the Union Jack.

"Bean rag" is slang for the flag flown aboard ship during meal hours. The men who used to help serve the meals were called bean jockeys.

Knot refers both to distance—a knot is one nautical mile, or 6,076 feet or 1,852 meters—and to speed. A ship making 30 knots is making 30 nautical miles per hour. It is improper to say "30 knots an hour" because knots *means* miles per hour. Since World War II all commercial and military aviation also measures speed in knots.

In sailing ships, speed was measured by putting a "chip log" over the stern. The "log" was at the end of a long line with knots tied in it at intervals. When it was put over, a "minute-glass" was started. At the end of a minute, the number of knots that had run out indicated the number of nautical miles—or knots—that the ship was making through the water.

Lanyard, any line made fast to something for the purpose of securing it, was originally spelled "land yard" and meant a piece of small rope—exactly three feet long—in other words, a landsman's measure of one yard.

Splice the mainbrace • During sea battles in square-rigger days, a vessels's rigging was a favored target. The first job following an engagement was to set up broken gear and repair sheets and braces. It was the custom, after the main braces were spliced, to serve grog to the entire crew. Today the meaning of this old custom has been twisted into a general invitation to "have a drink," or as the saying goes "splice the main brace."

The tie that binds • This expression of sentiment, regarding blood relationship or a similarity of ideals which hold people in a common bond, is generally believed to have been coined for the short chain which secures main and fore yards to their respective masts.

Chronometers, those precision instruments that navigators and quartermasters treat with tender care, are absolutely necessary in navigation. Until they were invented, navigators had no way of timing their celestial observations. The first successful chronometer was made by John Harrison, a carpenter. It was mostly wood, and weighed 66 pounds. The instrument proved itself aboard HMS *Centurion* in 1735.

Pelorus, the navigational instrument used for taking bearings, is named for a navigator who lived more than 2,000 years ago. Pelorus was the pilot who helped Hannibal evacuate his troops from Italy about 204 BC.

Dead reckoning is a method of navigation by which the position of a ship is fixed by plotting the distance steamed and course steered from the last well-established position. It was originally called deduced reckoning, then shortened to *ded* reckoning, but somewhere along the line someone thought the *a* had been left out of ded so he put it in, and that's how it's been ever since.

Amidships is frequently—and mistakenly—used to designate the waist of a ship. The term refers to a line running the length of a ship from bow to stern. Thus, the masts are stepped amidships.

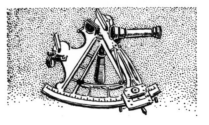

"Hog-yoke" was a slang term for the navigator's badge of office, the sextant used to determine position at sea.

Shackle comes from the old English *sceacel*, meaning fetter.

First Iron Ship • An iron vessel about 70 feet long was built in England in 1787. A sailing ship named *Vulcan* was launched in 1818. The first iron steamship, the *Aron Manby* was built in London and began operating in 1822. The first ocean-going iron ship was the *Great Britain*, completed in 1845. The first American ship built of iron was the USS *Michigan*, a side-wheeler, launched at Erie, Pennsylvania, on 5 December 1843. The following year the SS *Forbes*, a screw-steamer with an iron hull, was launched. The Navy's first steel-hulled ships, the *Atlanta, Boston,* and *Chicago,* were authorized in 1883.

Foul Anchor • It seems strange that the navies of the world should use as insignia the abomination of all good sailormen: somewhere back in early days a draftsman with more artistic ability than technical knowledge produced the well-known design which shows an anchor with its cable hopelessly fouled around the shank and arms. How such a design could win approval is beyond comprehension, but the fact remains that the sign of the fouled anchor has become an international emblem.

"Play the port anchor." In the games of Euchre and Five Hundred, the jacks in the deck of cards are named for the right and left bowers, the starboard and port anchors aboard ship.

Screws versus paddles • The first steamboats used paddlewhels. Similar wheels had been used long before that in water-powered mills on the banks of streams, and people understood how they worked. A screw propeller, turning completely under water, was something new. In 1839 the British Admiralty ordered a tug-of-war between HMS *Alert* (a screw steamer) and HMS *Rattler* (a paddle wheeler). Made fast to each other stern to stern, the ships steamed in opposite directions, and the *Alert* proved victorious.

"Sea dog" is an old timer.

Green oil and whistle steam. Old salts used to like to send a new man to the boatswain's locker to get some green oil for the starboard running light, or perhaps red oil for the port running light. If a man couldn't find either, he might be sent back for a bucketful of whistle steam.

Catheads were short heavy boomkins extending from the rail to port and starboard, near the bows. Secured slightly aft and above the hawseholes, they were used for bringing anchors aweigh, and were found on most ships until the beginning of this century, when they became obsolete. They were so named because in very early times they were surmounted with carvings representing cat's heads, the cat in those days being a royal pet.

Ditty box (or ditty bag) in which sailors used to keep small personal items, was first known as the "ditto box" because a man was supposed to have *two* of everything—spools of thread, needles, buttons, etc.

14

Clipper Ships • These sharp-bowed, fast sailing ships were an American development. The first clipper, *Rainbow,* was built in 1845; the last one put to sea about 1860. In that time more than 400 of the tall ships were built. They carried a cloud of sails; the *Sea Witch* could dpread more than an *acre* of canvas.

Names not on the chart • Old-time whalers sailed to the island of Owyhee. Later it was a part of the Sandwich Islands. Now it's Hawaii. When merchant sailors spoke of Dagger-rammer-rees, they meant Diego Ramirez Island; the proper name was too difficult for them. As late as World War II, charts showed Chosen; now it's Korea, and the port of Fusan is now Pusan. The big island south of Australia was named Van Diemen's Land until 1856, when it became Tasmania.

Pango is spelled Pago • People who hear sailors talk about Pango Pango will never find it on the charts of the Pacific; the place they are talking about is shown as Pago Pago. According to legend, when a first printing plant was set up there by missionaries, they had to spell the name as Pago Pago because they lost all the n's out of their type case.

Beheaded by a fish • When King Charles I of England put a heavy tax on the herring fisheries, a civil war resulted. That in turn resulted in Charles being beheaded.

Blue nose used to refer to people from Nova Scotia. It was also the name of the most famous fishing schooners on the Grand Banks. Now, in the Navy, it refers to someone who has crossed the Arctic Circle and qualified as a blue-nosed polar bear.

"Plankowner" is a man who has served aboard a ship since she was commissioned. In the old days when men slept on deck, many of them favored a particular spot where perhaps the planks were a bit softer, and some slept on such a spot until they felt they did own the plank. In the modern navy, it is a custom to give each man who helped commission a ship a "plankowner's certificate" when he leaves the ship for other duty. In some cases, ships give such men a small wooden "plank" with their name inscribed on it.

Solo Sailor • In 1895 Joshua Slocum, a retired sea captain sailed from Boston in the 33-foot *Spray,* on a one-man voyage around the world. He made it back to Newport in exactly three years and two days.

"Sack" is slang for bunk. A sailor who is sound asleep is "sacked out."

Reversed ranks • The reversal of the precedence of rank at naval and military funerals, whereby the seaman marches ahead of the commander, and the commander ahead of the admiral, is a practical demonstration of the teachings of humility as a cardinal virtue. It is based on a paragraph from the Bible which states ". . . the first shall be last, and the last first."

Big ocean waves are whipped up by the wind and their height in feet will usually be half of the wind speed in miles per hour —an 80 mile an hour hurricane will produce waves 40 feet high. But sometimes they are bigger. The SS *Queen Mary,* off Greenland, had her bridge, 90 feet above the sea, flooded by a giant wave. The biggest wave ever recorded was seen from the USS *Ramapo* in the Pacific on 7 February 1933; it was 112 feet high.

Cash for Columbus • Nothing could be more romantic than the story of Queen Isabella of Spain pawning her jewels in order to finance the voyage of Columbus to the New World, but it didn't happen. The Queen didn't put up a penny. Columbus borrowed the money from Luis de Santangel, keeper of the treasury of Spain. (*See* Finding an Angel.)

Santiago, Argentina (and probably half a dozen other places) celebrate the name of the Portuguese Saint Jago, and represents the results of poor spelling and pronunciation over the years.

"Dago," a disparaging nickname for Italians or Portuguese, is at least 400 years old. English sailors applied it to them after hearing them call loud and long on their patron saint, St. Diego.

Find an angel • This theatrical term has a nautical origin. It refers to the art of finding someone with more sentiment than business sense, who will provide the funds necessary to produce a "sure-hit" show.

It had its origin in the fact that Luis de Sant-Angel helped finance the voyage in which Columbus discovered America.

First Fort in America. The first structure built by Europeans in the Western Hemisphere was a fort, erected on the island of Haiti in December, 1492. It was made out of timbers from the wreck of Columbus' *Santa Maria,* which ran aground there.

Avast, meaning to stop or hold fast, comes from the Dutch *houd vast,* for "hold fast," and from the Portuguese *abasta,* "enough."

Cape of Good Hope, the extreme southern tip of the African continent, was first rounded by Phoenician sailors who took their ships from the Red Sea clockwise around the continent to the Strait of Gibraltar and back to Egypt about 600 BC. The Cape was rounded in an eastward direction for the first time in 1488 by Bartholomeu Dias, the Portuguese explorer. Because of the fierce storms there, he named it the Cape of Torments. Later King John of Portugal changed the name to Good Hope. (There may be something in the fact that the King didn't have to try to sail around it.) Until the Suez Canal was opened about a hundred years ago, *all* ships had to round the Cape, but afterward most steamships took the Suez shortcut—until Egypt closed the canal in recent times. The Canal is again open, but supertankers and many other types of ships are now so large they have to go around the Cape, and traffic is increasing.

Long pig • This sinister term originated with South Sea cannibals.

Until the coming of the white man, fish was about the only food other than fruit, roots, and berries, on the menu of the natives. The first explorers brought pigs, which increased in numbers to such an extent, that among the islanders the word "pig" became a synonym for meat. Naturally, a human victim prepared for consumption became "long pig."

Cape Horn "fever" was old-time slang for malingering when in far southern—and stormy—latitudes. Sailors developed sudden and mysterious maladies, planned to keep them in their bunks instead of working on deck in such rugged conditions. The fever was sometimes cured by a mate with a rope-end in his hand.

"Topsail buster" was old seagoing slang for a howling gale.

Great Lakes navigation began in 1679 when the French explorer LaSalle built a small ship named *Griffon* and sailed it in Lake Michigan. The first naval vessel on the lakes—and the first iron ship built for the Navy—was the side-wheeler *Michigan*, launched on 5 December 1843. The first vessel from overseas to operate on the lakes was the steamer *Madeira Pet*, which reached Chicago from London (via the Welland Ship Canal) after a voyage of 80 days.

"Spotted cow" was a British nickname for any German ships registered at Hamburg. The term was coined for Simon of Utrecht, Lord of Hamburg, whose banner bore the device of a dappled bull.

Typhoon • A severe tropical storm, or cyclone, in the Pacific. The name comes from the Chinese *tai fung*. A similar storm in the Atlantic is called *hurricane,* from the Spanish *huracan.*

Hooker was British term for certain small vessels trading between British ports and the Hook of Holland. The word now means any small or clumsy sea-going craft. It also is a common substitute for prostitute.

"Flying-fish sailors," in old Navy slang, were those who served in Asiatic waters. Those who served in the Med were known as "Sou-Spainers." In four-piper days, Asiatic sailors referred to those who were based in U.S. waters as "popsickle sailors."

Swiss Navy • Though it is a traditional joke among sailors that "I served my first hitch in the Navy of Switzerland," such a navy actually existed in 1799, when an English Captain Williams commanded a fleet of small vessels on Lake Zurich, in operations against the French.

Swallowed the Anchor • When a seaman uses this expression, he is not trying to belittle sword-swallowers or others of similar professions by claiming to have actually swallowed the right or left bower. He only means he has permanently quit the sea to take up a shore job, or to retire.

Air conditioned ships • Nowadays all ships have air conditioning, but it is a fairly new development. The first completely air-conditioned ships in the Navy were the heavy cruisers *Newport News* and *Salem,* built in 1947.

"Sparks" was the traditional nickname for the radio operator aboard ship. In the early days of wireless, there was always a big spark jumping across the open arc of a set when transmitting.

"Bird farm" is Navy slang for an aircraft carrier. The air control officer's station on the island of the carrier is called the bird cage. The platform where off-watch people watch landing operations is called vulture's roost.

"Airdale" is slang for a naval aviator, or "flyboy."

"Keep 'em Flying" was an Air Corps motto in World War II, but the Navy outflew the Air Corps. The USS *Enterprise,* in the war zone in 1945, kept planes in the air continuously, day and night, for 174 hours.

"Bomb alley" in World War II, British Navy slang for the Strait of Sicily; because of the almost continuous air-attacks on British shipping there. (*See* Torpedo Junction.)

Hawse holes were originally eyes carved or painted on the bows of ancient ships for the purpose of allowing the vessel to see if there were evil spirits ahead, and to veer away from her course until they had been left astern.

Through the hawse-hole • In the merchant marine, a sailor who advances from the rank of ordinary seaman to that of master or captain, is described as having "come in through the hawse-hole." On the other hand if he started as a cadet, trained as an officer, and reaches captain's rank, he is said to have "come aboard through the cabin portholes." (*See* Mustang.)

Tumble-home, the use of sloping sides in a ship's construction, is often thought to be so designed as an extra measure of strength or sea-worthiness. Actually, it was first invented to beat Suez Canal toll charges, which were based on a formula that muliplied length by depth by half the deck-beam.

As the deck-beam was reduced at least twenty-five per cent in tumble-home construction, the shipowner saved many a pretty penny until the Suez formula was revised.

Dinghy, the name of the smallest boat on a ship comes from India. In Hindu, *dinga* means boat, and *dingi* is the diminutive of dinga.

Jacob's ladder, the term for a boat ladder dropped over the side of a ship, comes from the Book of Genesis, where is described the dream in which Jacob saw a ladder ascending from earth to Heaven. The first time one climbs up the side of a ship at sea, with her pitching and the ladder swinging, it is easy to understand why it's named after the one Jacob saw.

Shove off is the order given to a small boat alongside a ship when it is ready to depart on any trip away from the ship. In small boats, a sailor standing in the bow actually does shove off the bow by pushing against the ship with a pole called a bowhook. Any and all leave-takings or departures are termed as "shoving off."

Lying on the oars • In the days before power boats, when several oarsmen propelled a boat, the boat carrying a senior officer was saluted by all the boat crew in the junior boat raising oars parallel to the water as they passed.

Ship with no ends • About a hundred years ago an Australian inventer drew up plans for a battleship with a circular hull. The Russians purchased the plans and actually built and launched such a vessel in 1876. With no bow or stern, it would seem that the only directions aboard such a craft would be outboard and inboard.

"Cutting a dido," said of someone who is showing off to extremes, was coined because the skipper of HMS *Dido,* an exceptionally speedy brig, used to show off his fast ship by sailing in circles around the slow old ships of the line.

"Cut of his jib," a phrase referring to a man's general appearance, is derived from the days when it was possible to distinguish French ships by their two small jib sails while British ships had one large single jib.

Submarines, whose nuclear missiles make them the most powerful ships in the world, had a puny ancestor. Cornelius van Drebel, a Dutch scientist, built the first submersible in 1622. It was made of wood, propelled by six men using oars, and actually did navigate, surfaced and submerged, on the Thames River at London.

"Hush-hush fleet" was the term the British applied to their first battle cruisers, because of the deep secrecy surrounding their building.

Deep Six means "throw it away, get rid of it." The expression comes from the leadsman taking soundings and shouting "By the deep six!" when the water is six fathoms, or 36 feet deep. Anything given the deep six is down where no one will get at it again.

Christmas tree is a lighted control panel of red and green lights, as on a submarine.

How Deep is the Ocean? It all depends on where one drops the sounding lead. Along the continental shelf, which may be from 30 to 800 miles wide, the sea slopes from the beach line down to 100 fathoms. Beyond the shelf, it drops down to two or three miles; the average depth of all oceans is about 13,000 feet. To date, the deepest known part of the ocean is Challenger Deep, in the western Pacific, where the bottom is 35,760 feet down. Only two men have ever ventured all the way to the bottom there; Jacques Piccard and Lieutenant Don Walsh made the trip in the *Trieste* in 1960.

21

Halliards are lines used to hoist sails and flags. The word comes from the order "Haul yards."

Gun Turrets • Revolving turrets for guns were invented twenty years before the Civil War by T. R. Timby of New York, who was then 19 years old. The world first became aware of the practicality of turrets when the Civil War *Monitor,* designed and built by John Ericsson, used her 2-gun turret against the CSS *Virginia* in the Battle of Hampton Roads. The *Virginia* had to turn around to aim her guns, but the *Monitor* merely rotated her turret. During World War II tanks and even airplanes carried rotating turrets. A turret on a World War II battleship weighed about 1400 tons—as much as a World War I destroyer—but through electric-hydraulic controls it could be trained from beam to beam, through 180 degrees, in 45 seconds.

Hospital Ships • The first hospital ship for the Navy, built as such from the keel up, was the *Solace;* commissioned in 1920 and decommissioned in 1946. During World War II the Navy had more than a dozen hospital ships in service. The first hospital ship used by the Navy was the *Red Rover,* a steamboat converted for such use during the Civil War. The job was fairly simple then; it consisted of not much more than painting "hospital ship" on the side of the craft.

Propellers for Ships • The idea of a "screw wheel" was first suggested by a Frenchman, Daniel Bernoulli, in 1752. In 1785 an Englishman, Joseph Bramah, patented a first propeller. The first practical propeller was made by John Ericsson in 1836. The British *Argo* was the first screw-propelled ship to go around the world; it took 121 days in 1853. The first screw-steamship that cruised at sea was the USS *Princeton,* launched in 1842. Twin screws were first used in 1888, and in 1905 and 1906 the first ships with three and four screws appeared.

Hull down • Said of a ship when it is just far enough beyond the horizon so that only masts and superstructure are visible.

Big ships • The British warship *Royal Harry* built during the reign of Henry VIII (1509–1547) was the first warship to attain a displacement of one thousand tons. The new nuclear-powered aircraft carrier, USS *Nimitz,* displaces over 91,000 tons. Jumbo tankers are better than twice that big.

Cruiser, a fast, well-armed ship, takes its name from the Dutch *kruise,* meaning to cross.

Pilot is a person qualified to take a ship into or out of harbor, through a canal, or through difficult and hazardous waters. The word comes from the Dutch *peil*—to mark with pegs, and *loth*—lead, which combine to form leadline. A pilot handles a ship within sight of land as compared to a navigator, who handles a ship at sea out of sight of land. Pilot has now come to include anyone who has the controls of an aircraft.

Oil-canning is an effect seen on the hulls of very thin-skinned ships, such as destroyers, where the plates are slightly dished in between frames.

Holystone • This was a block of soft sandstone, used for scrubbing wooden decks aboard ship, and so called because a man using a holystone usually worked on his knees, much as if he was praying. Holystones were banned in the U.S. Navy by General Order No. 215 of 5 March 1931, because they wore down expensive teak decks too fast.

Sidelights were white on both sides of ships until about 1830, when it became the practice to burn red on the port side and green on the starboard sides. Now, even aircraft carry red and green side lights.

Hawser • Any heavy line, five inches or more in circumference, used in towing or mooring a ship. The word comes from late Latin *altaire,* meaning raise, by way (probably) of old English *haelfter* which became halter, as used for "mooring" a horse.

British clipper racing • One of the greatest sea races of all time ended in London, England, on 6 September 1866 when the clippers *Taeping, Ariel,* and *Serica* arrived after a 14,060 mile run from Foochow, China. All three ships sailed from Foochow on 30 May and were nearly neck and neck the entire distance. *Taeping* docked in London at 9:45 PM; the *Ariel* docked 30 minutes later and the *Serica* only an hour and 15 minutes after the *Ariel.*

Red lead is anti-fouling paint applied to the hull of a ship. It is also a slang term for ketchup.

Bottled up, meaning to enclose or jam up, comes from the old custom of sailors carving miniature ships which were placed in bottles. So, saying "traffic was bottled up on the freeway" is a direct steal from the forecastle. There are hundreds of bottle ships in museums; probably some sailors had more fun getting the bottle empty than they did in putting the ship inside.

From Down South to Down Under • The SS *Edina,* which gained fame as a blockade-runner and dodged many Union ships during the Civil War, had a long life after the war ended. She was sold to some Australians who put her on a run between Port Melbourne and Geelong. (The illustrator of this book, as a boy, made many trips on her.)

Seven Seas • It's a common expression to say some old salt has sailed the seven seas, but how many people can name them? And why stop at seven? The best known seas are the Mediterranean, Caribbean, Philippine, China, North, Red, Black, White, Yellow, and Adriatic Seas. But there is also the Aegean Sea, Ionian Sea, Sea of Marmara, Sea of Crete, Coral Sea, Arafura Sea, Java Sea, Sulu Sea, Celebes Sea, Barents Sea, Norwegian Sea, Caspian Sea, Sea of Japan, Chukchi Sea, Laptev Sea, Kara Sea, Arabian Sea, Tasman Sea, Timor Sea, and the Dead Sea. All in all, there are at least 77 bodies of water around the globe named as seas.

Botany Bay is a port five miles south of Sydney, Australia. It was named by the famous navigator, Captain Cook, because of the great number of strange new plants found there.

Rover, a name for buccaneers (and innumerable dogs) was originally the trade name for riggers. They became known as rovers because they went from shipyard to shipyard as their jobs required, just as steelworkers and fruitpickers do now.

Fighting ferryboat • During the Civil War, the Union Navy was hard pressed for ships, and took over almost anything that floated and had an engine. One such craft was an unfinished ferryboat. She was sheathed with iron, named *Essex,* and met and sank the Confederate ironclad *Arkansas* after a hot fight.

"Taking a sight" Old Navy slang for thumbing one's nose, or "cocking a snoot" at an officer (discreetly, of course, and behind his back).

Careful with them cannons! The old frigate *Constellation,* in Baltimore, carries cannons, but couldn't even fire a cream puff out of them. The original iron guns cost too much to maintain, so they have been replaced with exact copies made of plastic. With 80 tons of weight gone with the cannons, the ship rode too high out of the water, so she was ballasted down with ingots of lead.

Grab the money and run • A Confederate naval officer who caused the Union as much grief and trouble as any other individual during the Civil War was Asbury Harpending. He secured a commission in the Confederate navy, so that he could fit out a fast schooner in California in hopes of capturing two ships, the *Constitution* and the *Oregon,* each supposed to be carrying a million dollars in gold. The schooner *Chapman* was all ready to go, but the USS *Cyane* and two boatloads of Marines got there first, and Harpending and his gang were hauled off to Alcatraz.

"Shot in the locker," meaning "something in reserve" comes from the days of sail when the British admiralty advised captains to "Keep always good reserve supplies in the shot-locker." Thus, in battle, there would be shot at hand to serve the guns. When one says "I haven't a shot in the locker," he means he's out of food, liquor, money, or whatever.

First Steamboat • Robert Fulton is generally credited with inventing the steamboat. His boat, the *Clermont,* began running on the Hudson River in 1807. But Fulton was behind the times; John Fitch built a steamboat that operated out of Philadelphia from 1788 to 1790, during which time it covered more than 2000 miles.

Panama Canal • The 50-mile canal across the Isthmus of Panama, completed in 1914, runs from Balboa on the Pacific side to Colon on the Atlantic side. Strangely enough a ship moving from the Pacific to the Atlantic winds up farther west when it reaches Colon than it was at Balboa, because the canal runs in a northeast to southwest direction. The canal cut the distance from New York to San Francisco by some 60 per cent.

First ship through the Panama Canal • The crane ship *Alex Lavalley* sailed through the canal on 7 January 1914. The first Navy ship to transit the canal, Pacific to Atlantic, was the collier *Jupiter,* 12 October 1914. The first transit from Atlantic to Pacific by naval vessels was made on 16 July 1915, by the battleships *Ohio, Missouri,* and *Wisconsin.* The first cargo ship through the canal was the SS *Ancon,* just after World War I began. The canal was formally opened on 12 July 1920.

Iron floats as well as wood, but in the early days of steamships, there was considerable doubt about it. British seamen protested in Parliament against sending iron ships to sea on the grounds that "Everyone knows that metal cannot float." Actually, a ship of iron weighs only half as much as one the same size made of wood, and a steel-hulled ship is 15 per cent lighter than one of iron.

First Atlantic Crossing by a Steamship • This record is attributed to the SS *Savannah,* which crossed the Atlantic in 1819. The trip took 29 days, and she used her engines for only three of them, so, although she was technically a steamship, the crossing was not made by steam; sails did most of the work. The next crossing by a steamboat was made in 1831, by the Canadian *Royal William,* in 19 days.

Anchor watch • Originally, an anchor watch was stood *only* when the ship was tied up in dock and her anchors stowed on deck. Then a watch was posted, "Lest," says the serious chronicler of early days, "some miscreants from ye other ships about, steal ye anchors while theye (the crew) sleepe."

Belay, meaning to cease hauling on a line, was originally *de-lay,* then corrupted to its present form.

"Dandyfunk" was a messy concoction of broken ship-biscuit smeared with molasses and probably the only desert ever served aboard the old wooden ships.

Catamaran comes from the Tamil *kattumaran,* a sailing raft of logs lashed together, which was developed in Ceylon. The double canoes seen in the Pacific islands by early explorers more nearly resembled the catamarans now being sailed in the United States. Catamarans are exceptionally fast and can ride heavy surf. Many large catamarans have crossed the Atlantic from Europe to the West Indies.

Admiral Penn of the Royal Navy, who conquered the island of Jamaica, actually had nothing to do with American history, yet one of the states is named for him. The wealthy admiral loaned money to the Duke of York and left a fortune to his own son, William. So, when William acquired from the Duke the land that is now Pennsylvania, it was not named for the Duke or William; the *Penn* in Pennsylvania stands for Sir William, the admiral.

Bowsprits are not the jib-booms of yachts and other small craft, as they are mistakenly called, but an integral part of a ship to which the figurehead is secured. Bowsprit comes from the old Saxon *sprit,* meaning "to sprout."

Bluff, meaning stout or hearty, also refers to the blunt bow of old sailing ships.

"Pelican" is slang for a hearty eater—a chow hound.

"Paddy Wester," was an old-time British term for a seaman whose lubberly behavior belied the rating recorded on his papers. In the 1880s Paddy West was a boarding house keeper in Liverpool who provided seamen to complete the crews for deepwater sailing ships. Men were hard to get, so Paddy rounded up misfits and outcasts in the slums, fed them, and turned them over to shipmasters. First he had them walk around a pair of cow-horns, so they could turthfully say they had "been around the Horn." Then, with cleverly faked certificates showing them to be fully qualified able seamen, Paddy West took the advance on their pay and shipped them out.

Old Navy refers to a period of time when things in the Navy were very different than they are now. Old timers talk about the Old Navy to impress anyone with less service than they have. When an old timer states that "Things ain't like they used to be in the old Navy," the proper reply is "No, and they never were."

Gun salutes were first fired as an act of good faith. In the days when it took so long to reload a gun, a ship which discharged her guns on entering port signified her friendly intentions. The first official salute fired by an American naval vessel was that rendered to the French in 1778, when John Paul Jones in the *Ranger* fired 13 guns—one for each state. As new states joined the union, more guns were fired in salutes, until by 1841 ships were firing 26-gun salutes. Finally, in 1875, Congress ruled that international salutes would be returned "gun for gun." At that time the British were firing 21-gun salutes, as they had since 1772, so the United States followed suit.

Gun salutes are fired in odd numbers . . . 1, 3, 5, 7, etc., because of the old superstition that uneven numbers are lucky. A national salute of 21 guns is fired on Independence Day, Memorial Day, and to honor the President of the United States or head of a foreign government. Salutes are fired at intervals of five seconds.

Siren, the steam or air powered warning signal used aboard ship, gets its name from the Greek *sirenes,* for "entanglers." In Greek mythology sirens were half women, half bird; they used their beautiful voices to lure sailors to destruction. In the oldest sea story known, Ulysses escaped the sirens by having himself lashed to the mast of his ship, and having all his rowers plug their ears with wax so they could not hear the songs.

SOS • The well-known radio call for assistance by a ship in distress does not stand for "save our ship." Early radio operators developed the signal because those particular letters were easy to identify. They consist of three dots, three dashes, and three dots, thus: · · · — — — · · · The same result can be achieved by sending the Morse equivalent for VTB (· · · — — — · · ·) or IJS (· · · — — — · · ·)

Sea chanties, no matter what one suspects, are not shacks down by the beach, but work songs sailors used to sing in the days before phonographs, radio, and TV. A chantey, pronounced *shantie,* was a work song. There were chanties for hauling on the sheets, hoisting anchor, manning the pumps, or whatever. A chanteyman sang the first line and all hands joined in on the chorus.

Dipping the flag • This international greeting at sea is a survival of the time when merchant ships were required to clew up their sails and wait for a man-of-war to send a boat to inspect their papers, or signal them to proceed. The flag salute was later adopted as a time saver. Merchant ships dip first, naval vessels answer.

"What-the-hell pennant." A most unofficial pennant, but one that many captains and yachtsmen have wished they could use. Over a speed flag, it means "what the hell is your speed," over a course flag it means "what the hell is your course?" and by itself, it just means *"What* the hell!!"

Skull and crossbones • Here's another belief gone by the board; it appears now that the "skull and crossbones" was not the death-flag of the pirates. When this insignia was flown it meant "deliver up all your cargo, you and your ship go free." When total death and destruction was planned the corsairs would hoist a red flag.

"Brass monkey" was the nickname for the dignified golden lion on the crimson field of the Cunard Steamship Company's house flag.

Sailing under false colors • This was first the subterfuge of pirates. These seagoing gangsters would fly the flag of some friendly nation in order to lull prospective victims into a feeling of security.

Pea jackets were originally made of Pilot cloth, and were named for the first letter of the material. The original spelling was P-jacket, not pea-jacket.

Hand-me-downs • Shoddy stores along waterfronts used to be filled with peajackets, oilskins, sou'westers, double-breasted serge coats hocked by hungry owners, or brand new seaboots at scandalous prices, all hanging on hooks high above one's head, and all requiring the use of stepladder or chair (and a stick with a hook on it) in order to be brought down for the prospective purchaser's inspection. So—"hand-me-downs,"

Bell bottom trousers, the wide-legged pants that went out with the jaunty white hats worn by sailors in the U.S. Navy until 1975, were cut with a flare in the legs because they were easier to roll up, as when a man was swabbing decks.

Slop chest was a locker carried on deep-sea ships from which the master of the vessel would disburse clothes to needy seamen during the long voyage . . . at a very excellent profit. The word slop is a corruption of the old English *sloppes,* meaning breeches or trousers.

Jersey, a woolen sweater, is supposed to have been named for one of the Channel Islands, the island of Jersey. Of course, Jersey also gave its name to a cow, so when you make out a chit for one Jersey, be specific.

Dungarees, the blue working clothes of sailors, take their name from a word imported from India—*dungri.*

Dunnage is a nickname for a seaman's personal gear, including his clothes. The term derives from the lumber known as dunnage, used in shoring up and dressing the cargo stowed in the ship's hold.

Uniforms for naval men were pretty much a hit-or-miss affair until in 1747 King George II of England ordered uniforms to be worn by all navy men, as a means of boosting their morale and improving their appearance. The first uniforms for the U.S. Navy, authorized on 5 September 1776, specified only the outfits for officers, and included blue coats, blue breeches, and red waistcoats with narrow lace. Enlisted uniforms were first authorized in September 1817; the winter outfit consisted of blue jacket and trousers and a red vest, all with yellow buttons, and a black hat. Rating badges for enlisted men were first worn in 1885.

"Feather merchant" is an enlisted man who retired and was recalled to active duty.

First Lighthouse • One of the Seven Wonders of the ancient world was the Pharos, or beacon light, erected at the harbor of Alexandria in Egypt by Ptolemy about 274 BC. The light has been stated to have been all the way from 375 to 475 feet high. It was finally destroyed by an earthquake in 1375.

The first successful lighthouse in modern times was the Eddystone Light, near Plymouth, England, built in 1756–1759 by John Smeaton. The first lights were candles. The Eddystone Light was replaced by a better structure after 120 years.

The first lighthouse in America was built on Little Brewster Island, in Boston Harbor, in 1716. Eventually there were hundreds of them along the U.S. coasts. Early lighthouses burned lard, fish oil, and finally kerosene; their lights were not very bright. Now, the light at the entrance to Buzzards Bay, in Massachusetts, puts out 9,000,000 candlepower.

Latitude and *longitude,* used by navigators at sea and in the air to determine their position, were developed by Arabian shipmasters in the 15th century. Longitude is now measured from the Prime Meridian at Greenwich, England, but in early times it was measured from Paris, London, Madeira, Teneriffe, and other places. Charts with four different scales for longitude were common.

Greenwich Time • Although Greenwich was established in 1675 as the international time center for mariners, it was not until the first World War, 1914–1918, that French navigators used any other than Paris time for their reckonings. Now the world is divided into 24 time zones. All navigation and communication is based on Greenwich Mean Time (GMT). GMT is shown as ZULU time in communications.

Compass • The magnetic compass was first used by the Chinese, as early as 2600 BC. An oddity of their compass was that the south end of the needle is marked, not the north end. Compasses were next used by the Arabs, in the 8th century AD, and finally reached northern Europe in the thirteenth century. Compasses used in the Mediterranean several hundred years ago had the East point marked, instead of North, as that indicated the direction to Mecca. Early compasses were marked in points—at first four, and eventually 32. The 360-degree compass was adopted by the U.S. Navy in the first years of this century, although the British Navy did not follow suit until during World War II.

Longest ship in the Navy, according to midshipmen at Annapolis, is the USS *Maine,* sunk at Havana, Cuba, in 1898. After the wreck of the ship was salvaged, years later, her two masts were erected as monuments, one at Arlington, Virginia, and the other at Annapolis. The distance between her two masts now is about 40 miles.

Long shot is a modern gambling term with an old nautical origin. Because ships' guns in early days were very inaccurate except at close quarters, it was only an extremely lucky shot that would hit the mark at any great distance, hence the inference of "luck" in the gambling term.

"Metal Men" is a derogatory term for retired enlisted men recalled to active duty. Because most of them were past middle age, wore gold hash marks, and were not so speedy in their movements as younger men, it was claimed of them that they had "silver in their hair, gold on their arms, and lead in their pants."

Junks, those remarkable wooden craft with bamboo battens for sails and which literally swarm in the bays and rivers of the Orient, were first mentioned in an Italian book printed in 1555, where they were called *guinche.* They are called *jonque* in French, *junco* in Spanish, *dschonke* in German; all these names come from the Malay *djong* which in turn comes from the Chinese *ch'uan* which means, as one might expect, boat. The design of junks has remained practically the same over centuries; one type seen around Shanghai looks much the same now as it did 2,500 years ago. A Chinese classic dated 2852 BC stated that boats were built by "hewing planks and shaping and planing wood." Despite their short stubby appearance, junks are excellent sea boats; some are now being imported to the United States for use as yachts.

Trim the dish, in the old days, was merely an order to the occupants of a small boat to seat themselves so it would move on a fairly even keel.

Yacht, the term for any vessel used for pleasure or recreation, applies whether it's a 30-foot day sailer, or a 250-ton diesel-driven air-conditioned seagoing palace with a swimming pool. The term comes from the Dutch *jaght* which was short for *jaghtschip* —ship for chasing. The English first used yacht as a name for pleasure craft about 1660. The first yacht built in America was called *Cleopatra's Barge*; she took to the water at Salem, Massachusetts, in 1816.

32

The Ladrone Islands, now known as the Marianas, were so named when Magellan's sailors discovered that the natives pilfered weapons, clothing, and anything else they could carry off. Ladrone is from the Portuguese *latro,* meaning thief.

First man around the world • Fernao de Magelhaes, better known as Ferdinand Magellan, is credited with being the first man to sail around the world. He led an expedition sent out by Spain in 1519; only one ship, under the command of Sebastian del Cano, returned to Spain in 1522. Magellan didn't complete the trip; he was killed by natives in the Philippines. But a man named Molucca Henry, who had been taken to Spain from the islands earlier by another explorer, and who sailed with Magellan as interpreter, was able to talk with natives when the expedition reached Leyte, so he had returned to the part of the world where he had first lived, and was in fact the first man to sail around it, having gone to Europe across the Indian Ocean and returned to the islands by crossing the Atlantic and Pacific.

Patagonia • This South American country received its name when Portuguese sailors noted with amazement the huge feet of the natives. They promptly nicknamed the Indians Patagones (*pata,* feet) (*gones,* big) and their country Patagonia.

Beachcomber, a term for a ne'er-do-well or loafer along the waterfront, originated in the islands in the South Pacific. It described the outcasts who had lost all ambition, and preferred to comb the beaches for a scant subsistence rather than earn a decent living by good honest work.

Gadget, the word used to describe any mechanical contrivance or device—or anything whose proper name can't be brought to mind instantly—was originally a proper nautical name for a hook. It comes from the French *gachette,* the catch of a lock.

Fresh water king is the man in charge of the evaporators, which produce the fresh water used aboard ship.

"Short timer" is a person whose term of service is nearly completed.

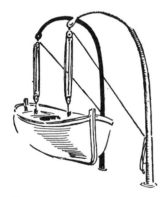

Davits, those small crane-like fittings used for hoisting boats, anchors, etc. aboard ship, were invented by, and named for, a Welshman with the name of David which, in Welsh, is pronounced *Davit.*

Stop all engines • In 1819 the SS *Savannah,* America's first steam-powered ocean-going vessel, crossed the Atlantic in 29 days. Literally thousands of ships followed her. But the last American ocean-going ship to carry passengers, the SS *Mariposa,* went out of service in San Francisco on 7 April 1978. All the big ships were put out of business by jet aircraft.

Steady steaming • The longest voyage ever made without any stops—from 16 November 1973 to 8 February 1974—was made by Commander Gerald P. Carr, Lieutenant Colonel William R. Pogue, USAF, and Edward G. Gibson, PhD, in the spacecraft *Skylab.* They flew around the earth 1214 times—a distance of 34,500,000 miles.

Derricks, whether cargo booms rigged to a kingpost aboard ship, or towering above an oil well, take their name from a 17th century hangman who plied his trade at Tyburn during the reign of Queen Elizabeth. Mr. Derrick invented a swinging boom for his gallows, with topping lift and boom step bracket, just as they are fitted today.

Round-the-world home run • Crew members of the submarine *Seadragon* played a baseball game in which the pitcher could throw south to all four bases, and a man making a home run ran east the whole way, around the world. The game was played at the North Pole in August, 1960, with half the diamond marked "today" and the other half "tomorrow."

Mate, whether First Mate in the Merchant Marine or Boatswain's Mate in the Navy, is derived from the French *matelot,* meaning sailor.

Captain comes from the Latin *caput,* for head. Captains were the highest ranking officers in the Navy until 1862.

Saved by a poem • The USS *Constitution,* better known as "Old Ironsides," was built in 1797. In her battle with HMS *Guerriere* on 19 August 1812, British shells bounced off her stout plank sides and, according to Moses Smith, sponger of no. 1 gun, someone said "Her sides are made of iron! See where the shots fell out!" The nickname of "Old Ironsides" soon became familiar. But in 1830 the ship was ordered scrapped. When Oliver Wendell Holmes learned of this, he wrote the famous poem that begins "Aye, tear her tattered ensign down! Long has it waved on high . . ." The poem was printed in nearly every newspaper in the country, and "Old Ironsides" was saved.

Far distant shores • Navy men on shore duty might get as far as a thousand miles from salt water, but in February 1971 Captain Alan B. Shepard, Jr., set a new record. He went to work on a base 250,000 miles from the sea—on the moon. A member of the *Apollo 14* mission, he was the first Navy man to walk on the moon.

Transatlantic cat • The first cat to cross the Atlantic by air was "Woppsie," a mascot of the Royal Navy. He rode the dirigible R34, which left Scotland on 2 July 1919 and landed in New York four days later. After four days at Mineola the R34, her crew of 31, two homing pigeons and the cat all flew back to England.

Land 'er sideways, Wilbur! • When the Wright brothers made their first flight at Kitty Hawk on 17 December 1903, the plane was airborne for 120 feet. Seventy years later they could have made several touch-and-go landings on the 1100-foot flight deck of the carrier *Enterprise*—or even landed athwartships, as the ship is 252 feet across at her widest point.

Shipbuilding record • The monitor *Monadnock* was laid down in Vallejo, California, by a private company, in 1876. After seven years the Navy took over the unfinished hull, and managed to complete it in another thirteen years. The ship finally went to sea in 1898. By contrast, the Kaiser Shipbuilding Company laid the keel of the Liberty ship *Robert E. Peary* on 8 November 1942, launched the completed ship four days and 15 hours later, and sent her to sea on 15 November 1942.

"Oil on troubled waters," an expression meaning an endeavor to pacify belligerents, comes from the old seagoing custom of discharging oil in rough seas around a disabled vessel, making it safer to handle rescue craft because the oil breaks up the waves.

Horn-pipe, the frisky sailor's dance, was named for the two instruments usually found aboard deep-sea ships, a horn and a pipe.

"Keep your shirt on," slang for "Don't get fighting mad," comes down from the Vikings, who gave us the term *berserk* because they used to fight with their shirts off.

Skylarking, now a good dictionary word, was first coined as a slang term to express the antics of young seamen who would scramble to the top masts of a ship and descend by sliding down the backstays, just as skylarks had a habit of soaring high into the air and then suddenly swooping to earth.

Different ships . . . different long splices, is an old Navy colloquialism meaning that there is more than one side to an argument, and more than one way of doing a shipshape job. It is a philosophy of tolerance everyone would do well to practice.

Berserk, meaning violently and destructively frenzied, comes down from the Vikings. It was their custom to tear off their shirts of mail and fight half naked. Hence the term *ber-serk,* meaning bare of shirt, as *serk* was the Norse word for shirt.

"Spinning a yarn," a term for story-telling (and particularly tall stories at that) was coined in days when sailors would be put to work taking old ropes apart to make yarn and other "small stuff." As this was the only shipboard task during which they could talk at will, the act of spinning yarn became synonymous with free and unrestricted conversation.

"Scuttlebutt" is Navy slang for rumor, gossip, or just plain bum dope. In sailing ship days, an open cask of water was set out on deck where men gathered for a drink and the latest "word." The cask was called a scuttlebutt; now drinking fountains with electrically cooled water are still called scuttlebutts.

Caulk off, pronounced "cork off," refers to sleeping, and comes from the fact that men sleeping on deck in sailing ships had their backs marked by the pitch used to fill seams after they were caulked or packed with oakum.

"Galley Yarn," in the merchant service, is a doubtful piece of information from the cook's department, with the same ring of uncertainty that is implied in the more familiar phrase "that's scuttlebutt."

Buttons on sleeves, when the sleeves belong to midshipmen in the British Navy, had to be sewed on athwartships at the orders of Admiral Nelson. In those days midshipmen had no pockets in their uniforms in which to carry a handkerchief; the buttons were so placed to discourage them from the practice of wiping their noses on their sleeves.

Sail Training. Steam has replaced sail in all the navies of the world, yet most naval officers still receive basic training in handling ships under sail. Midshipmen at the U.S. Naval Academy learn to handle knockabouts, yawls, and go on to big ocean racing craft. The U.S. Coast Guard sends cadets to sea in the 294-foot *Eagle.* The Portuguese training ship *Sagres,* pictured here, was named for the city in Portugal where Prince Henry the Navigator established the first naval war college in the world in 1415. Other sail training ships include *Gorch Fock* (Germany), the 375-foot four-masted bark *Kruzenshtern* (Russia), *Danmark* (Denmark), *Dar Pomorza* (Poland), *Nippon Maru* (Japan) *Libertad* (Argentina), *Amerigo Vespucci* (Italy), *Mircea* (Romania), *Tovaristsch* (Russia), *Esmeralda* (Chile), and *Sorlandet* (Norway). The oldest ship still used in sail training is the ex-Portuguese *Gazela Primeiro,* built in 1883 and now operated by the Philadelphia Maritime Museum.

Jack of the dust is an enlisted man in charge of the provision storeroom.

Sailing close to the wind • A sinister meaning has crept into this perfectly innocent and harmless phrase. When a man is making money by shady and suspicious methods, someone may say "He's making a fortune but —he's sailing awful close to the wind."

As a matter of fact, when a vessel is sailing close to the wind, she is merely pointing her nose as nearly into the wind as will allow headway, and is sailing close-hauled. There is nothing dangerous in so doing, and why the sinister element has been injected into the term is a mystery.

American clipper racing • In 1851, three fast clipper ships raced from east coast ports to San Francisco. The *Sea Witch* left New York on 1 August, followed by the *Typhoon* a day later. The *Raven* sailed from Boston on 5 August. The *Typhoon* reached San Francisco on 18 November, after a run of 108 days. The *Raven* arrived the next day, after sailing only 106 days. The *Sea Witch* made port the day after that, for a run of 111 days.

"Sea lawyer" is not a member of the bar, but a surly fellow who is forever arguing about anything and everything aboard ship, with a view to getting out of scrapes (and more particularly) out of work.

Anchor's aweigh! It's customary to note in the ship's log when an anchor is dropped, and when it's raised again, but this is not always done. The British warship *Centurion* anchored off Juan Fernandez Island one day in 1742, during the round-the-world cruise made by Commodore Anson between September 1740 and June 1744, but the *Centurion* never noted that the anchor was hauled in—the cable parted and she left it on the bottom. The *Centurion* had been scrapped and forgotten long before the anchor was seen again, that happened one day in 1882—*one hundred and forty years later!*—when the USS *Lackawanna* stopped at Juan Fernandez, anchored, weighed anchor, and brought up the one the *Centurion* had lost long before. The anchor is now in the Mare Island Navy Yard, at Vallejo, California.

"Frapped" is an old slang term for an inebriate. To "frap" a vessel was to pass cables under her keel and secure the two ends of the cable on deck, tightening them *a la tourniquet* by means of a capstan-bar.

This was done when bad weather had opened big seams by starting her strakes, and "frapping" literally tied the hull together as one ties a package. The slang term, of course, refers to the heavy weather a drunken man makes in his progress. How times change! Later, he was termed stinko, now he may be merely smashed.

Rocky Mountain Cruise • The first ship in the U.S. Navy to cross the Rocky Mountains was the destroyer escort *Brennan*. She was pre-fabricated at Denver, Colorado, then her hundreds of pieces were hauled to Mare Island, California, where she was assembled and launched. During World War II a dozen destroyer escorts and more than 200 landing craft, loaded piece by piece on long trains of flat cars, crossed the mountains from Denver to Mare Island.

Make the starboard side • The starboard side of a vessel is the traditional side to approach when making a visit by boat. This is because in ancient days ships were steered by a huge oar secured to that side, and a shipmaster, whose equally traditional station was close to the helm, could thus easily see who it was approaching his ship, and either welcome them or warn them off.

Cargo is a term derived from the Latin *carga,* meaning a load. It applies to anything carried by ships, barges, and aircraft.

Running her easting down • This old term refers to sailing in a particular area of the globe between South Africa and Australia. Vessels bound south to Melbourne or Sydney would round the Cape of Good Hope, and bear eastward on the long haul to the south-western corner of the land "down under." They sailed before the ever-prevailing trade winds in that quarter, and sailors spoke of this as "running her easting down."

Rope yarn Sunday • In the old Navy—up to about World War II—it was customary to knock off all work on Wednesday afternoon and give the crew a chance to scrub and wash clothes, mend them, and generally take care of personal affairs.

Anchor comes from the Latin *anchora.* Stone anchors were used by the Chinese as long ago as 2000 BC. Anchors range in weight from little ones a man can lift to the 30-ton monsters aboard the carrier *Forrestal.*

Island on the starboard side • The island on all U.S. aircraft carriers is on the starboard side, and not just because captains like to ride on that side. Propeller-driven airplanes have a tendency to pull to the left due to torque effect when power is suddenly applied, as when a plane making a carrier landing takes a wave-off. The Navy's first carrier, *Langley,* had no island, but when the *Lexington* and *Saratoga* were designed, it was only natural to put the islands on the right hand side, out of the way. Jet aircraft, of course, are not bothered by the torque effect. But traffic patterns are always to the left and islands are on the right, and it's too late now to change.

Futtock shrouds are the short shrouds extending below (and securing) the lower edges of the tops to the masts. Futtock is a corruption of the words *foot hook.*

Hammocks, which have now been replaced by bunks, were one of the discoveries Columbus made in the New World. Prior to that time, sailors slept on deck, anywhere they could find a soft plank. When Columbus reached the Bahamas, he and his men found the natives sleeping in nets called *hammacs.* Adopted by the Spaniards, the swinging beds were called *hamaco.*

"Donkey's breakfast." In old sailing ships, sailors slept on the deck, or on bare bunk boards, and later in hammocks. Any kind of a mattress was a great luxury. Because the first sea-going mattresses were usually filled with hay or straw, the term "donkey's breakfast" became a synonym for such beds.

Cure for seasickness, according to old salts, is to lay under a palm tree. Of course, by the time one gets ashore to a palm tree, he is no longer seasick. Perhaps the worst case of seasickness on record was that which afflicted a woman living in Cape Town, South Africa, who sailed to visit Europe just before World War I began in 1914. She was so sick on the trip that she spent the rest of her life— thirty-two years—in Europe, rather than go aboard a ship again.

"Son of a gun," a jocular familiarity now, is another expression that comes from the days when British sailors were allowed to take women to live aboard ship. If a baby boy was born aboard ship, and there was some uncertainty as to who his father might be, he would be entered on the muster roll as "Son of a gun."

40

Crow's nest, the name for the lookout station on the mast of a ship, was named for the cage Norse ships carried at their mastheads, in which some ravens were kept. When these sea warriors lost sight of land, they would release one of the birds. As it headed for shore with the uncanny instinct birds have, they would follow the course it took.

"The Eagle Screams!" Another way of saying that it's payday.

"White rats," in the old Navy, were men who tried to "bang ears" with the officers by telling them what was going on among the enlisted men.

Pigeons, those cosmopolitan birds that spend most of their time sitting around in parks and perching on statues, once were an official part of the Navy. The birds were used before and during the Spanish-American War to provide one-way messenger service from ship to shore. A bird based at Mare Island, California, was turned loose from the steamer *Alameda* over 400 miles at sea in May, 1897, and made it home. When seaplanes first operated, it was the practice to carry a pigeon on each flight. If the plane was forced down, the pilot sent it back to base with a note stating where he thought he was. When the USS *Langley,* the first aircraft carrier, was fitting out at Norfolk, the pigeon man sent his birds out every day to practice. Later the ship moved up the Chesapeake, and then, when the birds were sent out, they failed to come home. When the ship returned to Norfolk, all the pigeons were sitting on the dock, waiting for her.

Painter, the line fast at the bow of a boat, used either to secure it or tow it, gets its name from the French *pentoir,* meaning rope.

A-1 at Lloyds. When one is questioned as to his health, and state, that he is feeling A-1, he is borrowing an old marine insurance phrase. Lloyds, the greatest marine insurance company in the world, rated first class ships by registering them as A-1. Thus, the reply of A-1 means one is feeling absolutely at his best. (*See* Posted at Lloyds.)

"Loaded to the guards" was a slang term for one who had taken on more liquor than he could carry. It has reference to the load line, or Plimsoll marks, painted on all merchant ships to indicate the maximum load they can carry under various conditions.

Navy Day • Once a year the Navy holds open house for the public. That day, known as Navy Day, was inaugurated by the Navy League in 1922. The Navy League chose 27 October because that was the birthday of former President Theodore Roosevelt, who strove so diligently in promoting this country's modern Navy.

Lend a hand, in sea-going parlance, is a request for help. *Bear* a hand is a direct order.

Martinet, a term for any strict disciplinarian, was the name of a Frenchman, the Marquis of Martinet, who served in the French Army under Louis XIV, and carried discipline to extremes. The French still call the cat-o'-nine-tails a *martinet.*

Davey Jones is a corruption of Jonah, the Biblical gentleman who is credited with having stowed away in a whale for three days.

Mayday as used by aviators has no hidden political meaning. It is a distress signal, and comes from the French *m'aidez* which means "help me."

Fathom, used in measuring depth of water or length of line, is six feet. It comes from the Anglo-Saxon *faehom,* the reach of a man's outstretched arms.

Donkey engine, a small auxiliary engine used on deck in merchant ships, was so called because it replaced the animal which once powered hoisting gear along the waterfront.

"Liverpool pennant" was the nickname for the piece of string which a lazy sailorman would substitute for a missing button on his uniform. But Lord help him if he was found with such a "pennant" during inspection.

Suez Canal • The first attempt to link the Mediterranean and the Red Sea was made by an Egyptian Pharoah about 1800 BC. The present canal was completed in 1869 by the French engineer Ferdinand de Lesseps. It is 107 miles long and ranges from 500 to 700 feet across. Ships take about 15 hours to transit the canal. The first ship of the U.S. Navy to go through the canal was the *Palos,* on 13 August 1870.

Schooner, a word that defines any vessels of fore-and-aft rig, once had nothing to do with rig but referred to a speedy shallow draft vessel which literally "schooned"—or skipped —over the water.

By the Great Horn Spoon! This sea-going oath is supposed to refer to the constellation known as the Big Dipper, which some early mariners knew by the nickname of the "Great Horn Spoon." This name in turn referred to the days when feeding utensils were primitive and few. The wives and families of lowly people had small spoons carved from horn; the head of the house had a *large* horn spoon, which served the double purpose of helping the family from the common bowl, and by which he fed himself.

No seconds! Sailors love to eat, when the food is available. Perhaps an all time record was set by Captain Billy Booze, of Baltimore; he downed four dozen fried oysters, a half bushel of roasted oysters, nine soused pigs feet and nine glasses of Tom and Jerry at one meal, about 1900.

"Bully boys" were just ordinary sailors in Colonial times. The term did not refer to meanness or bad temper, but came from the well-known "bully-beef," the only kind of meat in their ration most of the time.

Uncle Sam • During the War of 1812, a meat packer in New York state, by the name of Ebenezer Wilson, worked with his uncle Samuel Wilson marking meat for government use. Because Samuel Wilson was known as "uncle Sam," the two men stamped meat cases with EW and US. People who knew them referred to such meat as belonging to "uncle Sam," and the expression soon came to mean the United States.

Collision mats are huge mats used to haul over a hole in the hull of a ship to prevent flooding. Also, slang term for pancakes.

Kids • In the old Navy, the shallow wooden (or metal) vessels used in carrying food from the galley to the mess table received their name from the boys whose job it was to help the cook by waiting on the seamen at mealtime. The boys were "kids" in the vernacular of the day, and the wooden trays were named after them.

"Strike-me-blind" was an old Royal Navy nickname for rice pudding with raisins. The inference was that one went blind looking for the raisins.

Seagoing cow • After canned or condensed milk was invented by Gail Borden in 1856, cows were no longer carried aboard ships. While Borden's primary object was to produce a sufficient and sanitary food supply for babies on sea voyages, the invention proved invaluable to infant and adult alike.

Grog, any mixture of alcoholic liquor and water, was first issued in the British Navy. The sailors drank straight rum until in 1741 Admiral Vernon suggested that the government could save money by diluting it, fifty-fifty, with water. As the Admiral always wore a cloak of *groggam,* a fifty-fifty mixture of silk and wool, his men nicknamed him "Old Grog." Jeering sailors at once nicknamed the new drink "grog" and the name has stuck to this day.

Drinking a toast, the term for drinking to one's health or in honor of someone, was coined in early days along the waterfront when it was customary to place a small piece of toast in the hot toddy and mulled wine popular with seamen of the time.

P's and Q's can stand either for pints and quarts, or feet and wigs. In sailing ship days when sailors could get credit at waterfront taverns until they were paid, the tavern-keeper marked up their bill on a board: P's for pints, and Q's for quarts. When it came time to settle up, it paid to "mind your P's and Q's." The other explanation—which sailors never were concerned with—was that in the court of Louis XIV of France, where people wore elaborate wigs, dancers were warned to "Mind your P's (*pieds,* or feet) and Q's (*queues,* or wigs)" to avoid having a wig fall off during a low bow.

Bucket of grog. In the old days, the Swedes knew how to make their holidays happy. It was the custom, aboard Swedish vessels, to place a bucket of grog at the wheel for whoever wanted a drink, between 24 December and 1 January. The records don't state what kind of course the helmsman steered.

Canteens aboard naval vessels are not as new as some people might think. The Romans had them too. The street called Via Quintana in Rome was the place where legionnaires went to buy whatever it was legionnaires bought when they went to town, in the days of Julius Caesar, and that's where the name canteen comes from.

Cheese it! No matter how one slices it, cheese is cheese. That is, until it's fired out of a cannon. Cheese actually won a naval battle in 1841, when ships of the Uruguay and Argentine navies met in battle. The Uruguayan fleet ran out of cannon balls, but, undaunted, the sailors loaded their guns with hard round cheeses and actually won the fight.

"Burnt offering" is British slang for any plain roast of beef or mutton.

"Admiralty ham" is a British nickname for canned fish.

"Water bewitched" was old time seagoing slang for weak tea. It went along with "shadow soup" which the cook made by letting the shadow of a beef bone fall on a kettle of hot water.

"Brown bagger," a slang term for someone who carries lunch to work, originally applied to married men on shore duty who brought lunch from home in a brown bag; now, anyone who takes lunch to the office "brown bags it."

"Pound and pint-ers" was a slang term for British ships when poor feeding aboard them caused Parliament to pass a law making it compulsory that every seaman be given one pound of food and one pint of tea or coffee at every meal.

Quarantine, the term for medical detention, comes from the French *quarant,* meaning forty. The first known case of a ship being isolated to prevent spread of disease took place at Marseilles, and the ship was detained for forty days—hence the name.

Scottish Engineers, it seems, have all left Scotland and gone to sea. Merchant seamen maintain that you can go aboard any ship, no matter what flag she flies, call down to the engineroom "Are you there, Mac?" and get the reply "Aye, mon!"

"Black gang" refers to the engineers who, in coal-burning days, *were* usually black with coal dust. They were also called bilge rats, or snipes.

Chop, as used in radio communications means, to transfer control from one command to another. Also, to indicate approval on a paper, from the Hindu *chap,* meaning stamp.

Cabin steward to skipper. After the San Francisco fire and earthquake in 1906, ships at the Mare Island Navy Yard sent fire and rescue parties to assist in disaster relief. The USS *Perry* kept sending men away until finally the only one left aboard was Sing Hoy, a Chinese steward. When all hands returned to the ship, it turned out that Sing Hoy had for several days been in sole command of a ship in the U.S. Navy.

Backing and filling. This seagoing term accurately expresses the motions of a sailing vessel holding her position without actually heaving-to. She would back her yards to spill the wind and stop forward motion; then, when tide and breeze tended to move her too far away, she would square her yards and run up to her original position.

Balloon Carrier. Long before airplanes were invented, the U.S. Navy had a carrier. During the Civil War an armed transport named *Fanny* launched an observation balloon to make observations of Confederate positions at Fortress Monroe, Virginia. The balloon reached an altitude of 2,000 feet.

Aye, aye is the proper reply by a junior to the order of a senior. It means that he understands the order and will carry it out. The expression is probably a corruption of the words *yea, yea,* which in Cockney accents became *yi, yi,* and from that it was a simple transition to *aye, aye.*

Row, Row, Row your Boat • They probably didn't sing all the way, because the trip took two months, but in 1869 two Norwegians, Frank Samuelson and George Harbo, climbed into an 18-foot boat in New York and rowed across the Atlantic to the port of Le Havre in France.

Careen comes from the French *carin,* meaning to turn over. In sailing-ship days, it was customary, on a long cruise, to run a ship onto the beach and careen her, first to one side and then to the other, to clean her bottom.

Ship that lit up a town • There was a severe drought in the Puget Sound area in 1929, and Tacoma, Washington, faced a power shortage. The Navy sent the big aircraft carrier *Lexington* to Tacoma where she tied up to a pier, spliced into the city electrical system, and for one month supplied power for the entire city.

"Charlie Noble" is a galley smoke pipe. The term probably originated with a British merchant captain named Charlie Noble who insisted that the cook polish the galley smoke pipe.

"Sling it over" is a colloquialism for "pass it to me." To seamen forever watching the loading or unloading of the ship's cargo by means of a net or sling, the latter was the obvious word to embody in a simple request like "sling me the salt."

Galley is the kitchen aboard anything from a 30-foot boat to an aircraft carrier. It is probably a corruption of *gallery,* the stone or brick platform amidships on Roman ships which mariners cooked their meals in the early days of sail.

"Rack" is slang for bunk. A sailor who is sound asleep is "racked out."

"Batten your hatch" was old Navy slang, meaning to "stop talking," "shut up," or even "button your lip." Once a hatch was battened down, it was tightly closed—nothing could get in or out.

Scrimshaw, the art of carving the teeth of sperm whales, comes from a Dutch word that meant a lazy fellow. On long voyages there was little for a man to do in his spare time, so men worked out intricate designs in the ivory they took from whales. The earliest known examples of American scrimshaw are dated 1821 and 1827.

Fleur-de-lys, the symbol that marks the north point on the compass, takes its name from the French word meaning "lily flower." The symbol resembles a lily, and it was used on the coat of arms for France at least six hundred years ago. The claim that the fleur de lys was adopted for the compass to honor Henry IV of France has no merit; early compasses had the letter T for *tramontana* (Italian for north) marking the north point, and some embellishment of the T turned it into a design which did resemble the royal French symbol.

"Salt junk" was old Navy slang for corned beef. As junk was the product of old rope unrove to be used in caulking seams, one has only to imagine the stringy quality of the salt beef to discover there was more truth than poetry in the name. It was also called salt horse when sailors found what might have been a piece of harness in the tub.

Hash mark is a stripe worn on the sleeve of an enlisted man to denote four years of service, the inference being that in such a period he ate a lot of hash.

So long comes from the East Indies *salaam,* meaning farewell.

"Hunky dory," a slang term meaning everything is OK, was coined from a street named *Honkidori* in Yokohama. As a sailor could find anything he wanted in that street, its name became synonymous for anything that is enjoyable or satisfactory.

"Chinese gangway" is one that leads forward instead of aft, the traditional fashion. A boat that makes a chinese gangway goes alongside a ship with its bow facing the stern of the ship, instead of in the customary bow-to-bow approach.

Joss, a Chinese name for god, comes from the Portuguese *Dios.*

Taksan, another word adopted from the Japanese *takusan* after World War II means the opposite of *skoshi,* or big, many, or a whole lot.

"Golden dragon" is a sailor who has crossed the International Date Line and entered the "Realm of the Golden Dragon."

Skoshi, or *skosh,* is a fairly recent addition to military slang, picked up from the Japanese *sukoshi* after World War II. It means little, few, or not much.

Bumboat is any small boat, used by waterfront merchants or natives to carry provisions, vegetables, cheap souvenirs, and sometimes illicit items, to ships in a harbor or roadstead, where they are sold to the crews. The name is probably a corruption of "boom-boat," because they were sometimes allowed to tie up to a boat boom. The Gilbert and Sullivan operetta HMS *Pinafore,* has as a principal character "Buttercup, *a bumboat woman."*

Wallop, now a forceful blow, was once a fighting admiral. When the French burned the town of Brighton, England, back in the 1500s, Henry VIII sent Admiral Wallop to teach the French a lesson. He so thoroughly wrecked the French coasts that ever since, any devastating blow is referred to as "an awful wallop."

"It'a an ill wind." The old saying "It's an ill wind that blows nobody any good" was originally a nautical expression exclusively. It meant that no matter which way the wind blew, some ship must profit from its direction.

Took the wind out of his sails. This expression, meaning to best an opponent in some argument, comes from sailing ship days. Originally it was a maneuver by which one vessel would pass close to windward of another, thereby keeping the breeze from the other's sails and making him lose way.

Overwhelmed, meaning crushed or defeated, is from the old Anglo-Saxon *whelman,* which means to turn a vessel completely over.

Army at sea • Until 1546, seamen were merely hired to work a ship, the supervision of battle at sea was handled by a general or some other army officer.

Battle of Santiago, between American and Spanish forces, was fought off the coast of Cuba on 3 July 1898. As the Spanish fleet left the harbor, American forces took up the chase, and in four hours the entire Spanish fleet was sunk or run ashore. Spanish losses were 350 killed and 150 wounded. Only one American sailor was killed. It was during this fight that sailors on the *Texas* cheered as a Spanish ship burned, and Captain John Philip called out "Don't cheer, boys. Those poor fellows are dying!"

Christening ceremony • When a ship is launched, she is officially named by a sponsor who breaks a bottle of champagne over the bow of the ship as she says "I christen thee . . ." Wine was not always used. When the *Constitution* ("Old Ironsides") was launched, water was used but the ship refused to move. Then a bottle of Madeira wine was used, and the launch was successful. The first woman sponsor of a naval vessel was "a Miss Watson of Philadelphia," who christened the USS *Germantown* on 22 October 1846. The only woman not a U.S. citizen, to christen a U.S. ship was Lady Dixon, wife of Australian Minister Sir Owen Dixon, who christened the USS *Canberra* in 1943. The ship was named for HMAS *Canberra,* lost in the Battle of Savo Island.

"Chief Housemaid" was old British Navy slang for the first lieutenant, because that officer was responsible for the cleanliness of the ship between decks.

First Lady of the Seas • The SS *United States,* the world's fastest luxury liner, made her first Atlantic crossing in 1952 in the record time of three days, ten hours and 2 minutes, cutting the 14-year old record of the *Queen Mary* by ten hours. She averaged 40.98 miles an hour. In 17 years of service, the *United States* made 726 Atlantic crossings, and carried a million passengers.

Best girl's on the towrope is an old Navy slang term descriptive of "fair weather and easy going," on the homeward passage. If the ship was making good progress, the seamen would say "Ah! the best girl is on the towrope."

"Bloody," when used by Britishers, can mean almost anything, good or bad, depending on the tone of voice, but it usually serves as a substitute for damned or extraordinary. Once upon a time it was a pious oath: "By our Lady!" Poor pronunciation and hurried exclamations shortened it to "By oor Leddy," then to "B'oor Luddy," and finally to "Bloody."

First Family Allowance • In the thirteenth century Irish shipmasters were compelled by law to provide for the needs of the families of every man in their crews. Whether or not it included "his sisters and his cousins and his aunts" it was a tall order anyway.

Buoy, for any knid of float used to mark a channel or carry a navigational aid comes from old English *boye,* a float.

Unlucky Friday • The reluctance of seamen to sail on Friday became so common that many years ago the British government decided to take strong measures to prove the fallacy of the superstition.

They laid the keel of a new vessel on Friday, named her HMS *Friday* and launched her on Friday. Then they placed her in command of one Captain Friday, and sent her to sea on Friday. The scheme had only one drawback—neither ship nor crew were ever heard of again.

House flag • The flags of the various shipping companies are known as "house-flags" because the device borne on such flags is the insignia of the company or house which operates the ships.

Their origin dates back to medieval days, when Crusaders, off to the Holy Wars, each carried on his ship a banner showing the crest or coat-of-arms of the house or family to which he belonged. Modern merchant marine officers wear an enamelled replica of the companies' flag in the badges on their caps.

Clawing off is old sea-going slang for anyone stuttering and stammering, trying to side-step an embarrassing question or argument. Its significance had reference to the back-breaking task of kedging (clawing) sailing ships past headlands to catch a breeze. The task itself consisted of conveying a kedge anchor a cable's-length ahead of a becalmed vessel, dropping it over, and rowing back to the ship. Then, with the cable bent onto a windlass, men heaved the ship forward to the kedge, and repeated the operation until they encountered the desired breeze.

"Jack Tar," as a nickname for sailors, comes from the fact that in sailing ships, the rigging was tarred and men had the stuff on their hands and clothes. Sailors also wore canvas breeches and coats coated with tar to make them waterproof.

Railroad pants were an officer's dress trousers with stripes of gold braid down the outside seams.

Side boys • In the British Navy a couple of centuries ago, visiting officers were hoisted aboard in a basket if the weather was too rough to rig a gangway. As officers gained rank—and weight—over the years, it took more men on the line to haul them aboard. Now, men detailed as side boys merely take station at the quarterdeck—or plane ramp—and salute an officer making an official visit. At some naval air stations in recent years, sideboys have been women.

Mufti, as "in mufti," means dressed in civilian clothing. The word comes from *muf-tee,* a West Indian word meaning a civilian.

Idlers are members of the ship's company who stand no regular watch. It does not include the toil-worn members of the medical staff, the steward, messboys, and others who work on a different schedule.

Nelson's Blind Eye • Admiral Viscount Horatio Nelson, the great British sailor, was blind in his left eye. When, during the Battle of Copenhagen on 2 April 1801, his senior officer ordered him to break off the action, Nelson put his telescope to his blind eye and said "I really do not see the signal." But when a statue of Nelson was erected in Trafalgar Square in London, it shows him as blind in the right eye instead of the left.

Lucky bag was a locker aboard ship where lost articles of clothing or other personal gear were turned in. Every so often, the lucky bag was opened and those who could identify their property were able to reclaim it. But there was a catch—anyone claiming gear from the lucky bag got a few lashes with the cat-o'-nine tails to teach him not to lose anything again. Ships still have a place where lost or misplaced gear is turned in, although no one is flogged any longer for recovering his gear. Probably the most famous Lucky Bag in the Navy is the year book prepared by midshipmen at the U.S. Naval Academy.

Seven bells are never struck in the second dog-watch aboard British naval vessels. In 1797, British sailors planned a mutiny; the striking of seven bells in the second dog-watch was to be the signal for action. The plot was discovered and the mutiny was quelled by making certain that the signal was not sounded. The Admiralty decreed that never again should seven bells be struck in the second dog-watch.

Sweating the glass, or flogging the clock, was an old scheme by which the sand in the hourglass was hurried down by shaking it (or, at a later date, the hands of the clock were put forward) in order to shorten the time of the watch on deck.

Sun's over the foreyard is an old time expression meaning "It's time for a drink." In days when drunkness was common aboard ships, the British Admiralty ordered that "no officer shall partake of liquor until the sun shall have risen well above the foreyard." The order failed to specify what to do on cloudy days.

Eight bells means eight o'clock. This all landlubbers know; not many of them know that it can also mean four o'clock and twelve o'clock. In days when time was marked by a 30-minute glass, the boy whose job it was to turn the glass struck the bell once the first time, twice the second time, and so on through a four-hour watch, after which the routine started all over again. It was customary in the old Navy to measure time by "glasses," meaning half-hours; ". . . we then fired our guns for nearly three glasses."

"*Dead Marine,*" a slang term for an empty bottle, was originated by the Duke of Clarence. At a banquet aboard ship in his honor, he ordered the removal of empty bottles by saying "Take away those dead marines." A Marine major objected to calling the bottles dead Marines, and the Duke explained: "They are fine fellows who have nobly done their duty, and, if filled once more, would be willing to do so again."

The Marines Have Landed! • That news has made many headlines over the years. The expression was originated by Richard Harding Davis, covering the Marine landing at Vera Cruz, Mexico, in 1914. His complete statement was "The Marines have landed and the situation is well in hand."

Marines • The first Marines were British, and were known as "The Duke of York and Albany's Maritime Regiment of Foot." In 1664 there were 1,200 of them. The first American Marines were enlisted at Tun Tavern in Philadelphia on 10 November 1775—*before* the U.S. Navy was officially organized. That date is still celebrated as the birthdate of the Marine Corps.

Toasts while seated • British naval officers have the privilege of remaining seated when drinking a toast to the King—or Queen.

This is because when Charles the Second of England was rising to drink a toast while dining aboard ship, he bumped his head on a low beam. He then decreed that from that time on, officers drinking the royal toast could remain seated without incurring regal displeasure.

"Leatherneck" • A U.S. Marine. The Marine uniform, in 1812, included a leather-lined collar which looked military but was uncomfotable; it was abolished nearly a hundred years ago, but the term is still used.

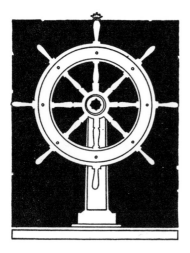

King spoke, on a ship's steering wheel is that one which, when standing vertically, indicates the rudder is amidships. The name comes from the old custom of decorating that spoke with a crown in honor of the king. Sometimes the king spoke is given a different shape, so it can be detected in the dark. With the advent of rudder angle indicators, king spokes were no longer necessary.

Homeward bound stitches • In the old days sailors were particularly neat with their sewing. Careless sewing was referred to as "homeward bound" stitching, the idea being that it was only a temporary makeshift until port was reached, when mother, wife or sweetheart could be counted on to finish the job properly.

Sunday to Saturday • If a ship has only one mast, it's called the mainmast. Most sailing ships had three masts, named fore, main, and mizzen. In the late 1800s there were a few schooners with four masts, some with five or six, and one—the *Thomas W. Lawson*—with *seven* masts. Technically, her masts were, from forward aft, fore, main, mizzen, jigger, driver, pusher and spanker. But many people could not remember which came first, so the masts were also named for the days of the week. Sunday was forward, Saturday was all the way aft, and Wednesday was back about where the galley deck house stood.

"Locker stick," a mythical piece of equipment used by a sailor trying to jam all his gear into a tiny locker.

Stork ship • During 26 years of service on the North Atlantic run, the SS *Independence* had 1500 babies born aboard ship while at sea. All of them were brought safely ashore.

Frosty flight deck • Inventors have come up with many screwball ideas for ships, but the wildest of all was the plan for an aircraft carrier built of ice, in World War II. The ship was to be 2,000 feet long, 300 feet wide, and 200 feet deep. She was to operate in the cold north Atlantic, but carry refrigeration equipment to keep her from melting in case she had to go south. The ice ship was estimated to cost $70,000,000, but it was never built. Possibly someone got cold feet.

Charts. The first charts known to be used by European seamen were made by the Italians in 1351, and were called *portolani* or *portolans.* They were usually printed on sheepskins. The U.S. Navy began printing charts 1883. Now, more than thirty million are produced every year.

Cuban souvenir • During the Spanish-American War of 1898, American troops staged a landing at a small Cuban town no one had ever heard of before. But the locals there treated some of the officers to a cool, refreshing drink, and when they came home, they brought back the recipe and the name of the town where they found it. You celebrate that landing in Cuba every time you order a *daiquiri.*

Blueprints by the mile. The first ship built in America, back in 1607, was a little 30-foot craft called *Virginia of Sagadahock.* Shipbuilding was simple then; men cut some logs, trimmed the timbers to shape, put them together, and there she was. In order to build the Navy's nuclear-powered aircraft carrier *Enterprise,* some 350 years later, it was necessary to draw over 16,000 various plans and produce 2,400 miles of blueprints—enough to sink the little *Virginia.*

Rudders at the stern of a ship first made their appearance in the 13th century. Prior to that time, they were fitted on the starboard quarter. A ship named *City of Elbing,* in 1242, was first to sport the new-fangled steering arrangement.

Quarter-deck voice • Contrary to popular belief, "quarter-deck" voice does not refer to the amount of noise an officer can make in giving orders. It is an old expression coined to describe the voice of authority. The term carried also the suggestion of the cultured or educated voice of an officer as compared with the uncouth tones of an ordinary seaman.

"Squared away," meaning one is in a satisfactory position for whatever has to be done next, is another phrase borrowed from square-rigger days. When a square-rigged ship braced her yards right across the ship to run before the wind, she was "squared away."

Mother Carey's chickens are stormy petrels—small birds seen flitting over wave crests, and often, it seems, just before a storm. The name of Mother Carey comes from *mata cara*—dear mother; it refers to the saint who protects sailors at sea.

Oldest Sea Story • The oldest known tale of the sea, dated 2500 BC, is housed in the British Museum. Written on papyrus, it recounts a terrific struggle between a sailor and a sea serpent.

"Topside sampan" was Navy slang for the old WW II Catalina seaplanes.

People by the planeload • In 1949 the Martin flying boat, *Marshall Mars,* set a record by carrying 308 people, including the crew, from San Diego to Alameda, California. That record was exceeded in 1975 just before the fall of Saigon, when a Navy Lockheed C-130 flew from Ton Son Nhut airport to Thailand with a total of 452 people on board. The plane was so crowded there were 32 people in the cockpit.

Victory parade • The smart gestures and prancing gait of modern drum majors, and majorettes, are a relic of the days when seamen ashore after a naval victory were encouraged to march along shouting and waving their arms (and side-arms), leaping into the air to express exuberancy, and work up a little public enthusiasm for their government's war efforts.

"Irish pennant" is any piece of line or rope not properly secured and hanging in an untidy manner, or an unwhipped rope end.

Rescue the Perishing. That might be the U.S. Coast Guard's second motto. Every year the Coast Guard answers more than 65,000 calls for help, and rescues more than 4,000 people.

"Riding the bear," in the old Navy, had nothing to do with a circus. The bear was a box-like frame filled with holystones, which seamen hauled back and forth along wooden decks for an extra slick-up.

"Raise the wind," a slang term for raising funds for some specific purpose, dates back to the days when a shipmaster went to a witch or fortune-teller and paid her for assurances that fair winds would enable his vessel to make a successful voyage.

Tarpaulin muster was old Navy slang for helping a shipmate in distress. A tarpaulin was rigged as a catch-net and the crew would file past, contributing whatever they could spare to help their financially embarrassed comrade.

Chit is a requisition, IOU, or note. It is derived from the Hindustani word *chitti,* meaning marked.

Admiral's "eighth" refers to the old practice of paying prize money to admirals in the Royal Navy for all ships captured by the fleet under their command. The admiral got one-eighth of the value of all captured ships, as allowed by the prize courts, whether he was present at the time or not.

Sterling silver was once called "Easterling silver," because a certain tribe on the Baltic Sea insisted on being paid in cash, or silver, for their goods instead of by the usual system of barter. Seamen carried money especially for that trade, and called it "easterling money" or "easterling silver," from which *sterling* was derived.

Press-gang "Pets." In the days when press gangs operated, seamen engaged in dockyards or sail lofts were given papers exempting them from being "pressed" into service. As press-gangs were naturally anxious to get ex-seamen rather than landsmen with no experience, a press-gang "pet" was anyone in the exempt classification who forgot to carry the necessary papers because, despite his protests, he could be shipped out for a cruise.

"Doctor discharge" is an old slang term for a fake discharge. In the last days of sail, when experienced sailors were at a premium, ordinary seamen would pay the ship's cook to alter their discharges into the higher rating of A.B.

As the cook was traditionally called "Doc" aboard ship, the faked tickets became known as "Doctor" discharges.

"Retread" is a man, either officer or enlisted, recalled to active duty after having been released to inactive duty in the reserves.

Knows the ropes • This phrase now indicates that a man is an expert, but originally it meant exactly the reverse. In the days of sail, when "He knows the ropes" was written on the discharge papers of a seaman, it meant that he was a novice, but did know the names of the principal ropes aboard ship.

Ensign, the lowest rank of commissioned officer in the Navy, comes from the old Norman *enseigne.* It was adopted by the British Navy in the 16th century, and by the U.S. Navy in 1862 to replace "passed midshipman."

Admiral comes from *amir-al-bahr,* an Arabic expression meaning "commander of the seas." The first officer in the U.S. Navy to be appointed to the rank of rear admiral was David Glasgow Farragut, who assumed that rank on 16 July 1862. Only one officer ever held the rank of Admiral of the Navy—that was George Dewey, the hero of the Battle of Manila Bay, who had the rank conferred on him on 2 March 1899. The first five-star "fleet admirals" in the Navy were Ernest Joseph King, William D. Leahy, and Chester W. Nimitz, whose appointments were ratified on 15 December 1944. John Paul Jones once served in the rank of admiral, but only in the Russian Navy.

Commander was first used as a designation of rank in the Navy in 1838, to replace "master commandant." It comes from *commandeur* which was introduced in the British Navy by William III (1553–1584).

Crew originally referred to the men in a ship's company, but now takes in the flight crew of an aircraft, the people who move scenery in a theater (stage crew), the men who handle a freight train (train crew); and those who dismantle buildings (wrecking crew). The word comes from the French *creue* meaning augmentation, or reinforcements.

Ship's master, referring to the officer who commands a merchant ship, originated during the Punic Wars (268–202 BC) between Carthage and Rome, when such men were titled *magestis navis,* Latin for master of the ship.

"Old Man" • Captain, as applied to an officer in the Merchant Service, is a courtesy title only. His official rank is that of Master Mariner . . . and he's generally called the "Old Man." In the Navy the commanding officer of a ship is called Captain, even though he may be only a lieutenant. Officers and men sometimes call him the "Old Man," but not when he's around.

Skipper, meaning the captain of a ship, comes from the Dutch *schipper* which means the same thing.

Boatswain, pronounced "bosun," refers to the mate, warrant officer, or petty officer in charge of boats, rigging, and ground tackle aboard ship. In Old English, *swein* meant servant or keeper. The later English term was *bote-swayn.* In the 17th century, British ships were required by law to carry three boats, named (1) *the boat,* (2) *the cock,* and (3) *the skiff.* The men in charge of them were called boatswain, cockswain, and skiffswain.

Chaplain. According to legend, St. Martin once divided his coat with a poor begger one bitter day. Somehow, the coat remained miraculously preserved and finally became a holy banner for the King of France. It was hung in an oratory that was named "the chapelle," and the custodian charged with its safekeeping was called the chaplain. The term now applies to any minister, priest, or rabbi in military service.

"Holy Joe," a traditional shipboard slang term for a preacher, is generally supposed to have been coined for Joseph Smith, founder and Prophet of the Mormons—the Church of the Latter-Day saints. Navy chaplains are more commonly called "padre," Latin for *father.*

Purser refers to the officer, aboard a merchant ship, who handles the accounts, pays bills and wages, etc. The term probably comes from the Latin *bursa,* or bag; before paper money and credit cards came into use, money aboard ship was carried in leather bags.

Master mariners • There were no licensed masters in charge of ships until the year 1450, when Charles the Fifth of Spain signed a law making it compulsory for a shipmaster to carry a certificate recording his qualifications for the job.

Boatswain's pipes were first used in early Roman and Grecian galleys; their shrill tones set the pace for slaves at their oars. During the Crusades, English bowmen were piped on deck with the boatswain's pipe, or "call." Shakespeare mentioned the pipe in *The Tempest.* A boatswain piping with his right hand is permitted to salute with his left hand.

Commodore is applied, as a matter of courtesy, to any officer commanding a squadron or flotilla of destroyers or smaller ships. It was first used in 1862, abolished in 1899, revived for World War II. The title was first introduced into the British Navy by William III.

East Indiamen • The big ships of the British East India Company (the "Honorable John" Company) came into prominence early in the nineteenth century, although smaller ships of the same line had, of course, been trading to India years before that time. They were huge, compared to the earlier vessels, and were really a compromise between a man-o'-war and a merchantman.

They carried both passengers and cargoes. What is more to the point, they were heavily armed and carried crews trained to fight. This made them almost invincible to the pirates who then infested the sea lanes.

They were such a source of pride to the British public that young men of good families preferred service under the "Honorable John" house flag, to a commission in the Navy.

"Lime-juicer" was a nickname for the old British sailing ships which were required by law to carry lime juice, which sailors had to drink to avoid scurvy. Consequently, British sailors became known as Limeys. No one in those days had heard of vitamin C, but that's what it was all about; lime juice contained the stuff and a pint a day kept a man's teeth from falling out.

Mine warfare, which reached its height in World War II when all the warring nations laid hundreds of thousands of them from surface ships, submarines, and aircraft, had its beginning hundreds of years ago. During the seige of Antwerp in 1583, small boats termed "infernals" or "fire ships" were filled with explosives and inflammables and floated in among enemy ships. The "torpedoes" that Admiral Farragut so heartily damned at the Battle of Mobile Bay were just a primitive form of mine. Thirty years after World War II ended, a mine shows up once in a while, and can be just as dangerous as when it was put in the water for, as mine experts say, "Mines never surrender."

"Torpedo Junction" was a nickname for the area of the sea off Guadalcanal in the Solomon Islands, where fierce battles between US and Japanese forces in the early part of World War II sent many ships to the bottom. Because so many ships were sunk there, it was also called Ironbottom Bay.

Balaclava helmets. In the old British Navy, it was a common stunt to cut the foot off a woolen sock, and wear the leg of it pulled over one's head in cold weather. It was called a "Balaclava helmet" because British soldiers started the practice during the Crimean War; the Battle of Balaclava was fought during that war, on 25 October 1854.

Unsinkable cat • When the German battleship *Bismarck* was sunk early in World War II, British sailors rescued the ship's mascot, a black cat, and named him Tom Bismarck. When his new ship, the *Cossack,* was torpedoed, the cat was one of the survivors. Transferred to the *Ark Royal,* the cat got sunk again when she was sent down, but again he was rescued. That time the British put him on shore duty; he was sinking too many ships.

The Silent P • Minecraft in the Navy used to be named for birds. One of them was called *Ptarmigan,* a name in which the first letter is never pronounced, and so acquired a most distinctive nickname.

60

Firecrackers, invented by the Chinese, were first used in America in 1787 when the merchant ship *Grand Turk* returned from Canton with a cargo of silk, tea, and the noisy fireworks.

Taken aback • When a sailing ship was taken aback (by reason of sudden squalls or faulty steering) she was momentarily helpless and in a position of great peril. With her sails blown back against the masts, she was in grave danger of being dismasted and transformed into a derelict. Only the smartest action by skilled seamen could save her.

In modern language, *taken aback*, describes the feelings of a person jolted by unpleasant news. He is taken aback; his mental equilibrium is upset, and for a moment he is unable to act normally.

"Deck ape" is slang for a man working on the topside of a ship. Such a man is also known as a swab jockey.

Tonnage originally had nothing to do with weight or displacement of a ship. It merely indicated the size of a ship by the number of *tuns* or barrels of wine she could stow in her hold.

"Dutch courage" • This is defined as courage inspired by drunkenness—quickly inspired heroism. It was coined to describe a custom of the old Netherlands Navy, when it was the practice to serve gin or schnapps to the gun crews of ships before going into battle.

"Mainsail Haul" was a nickname for loot or booty taken in a fight.

Mutiny • In 1842, the USS *Somers* sailed on a training cruise with 130 new midshipmen and apprentice seamen. When Captain Mackenzie heard that a mutiny was being planned, he ordered three ringleaders seized. Tried by court martial, they were found guilty and sentenced to be hung. Mackenzie was later tried by court martial, and exonerated. But of the officers who tried the mutineers, one was killed later while riding a horse, one died of drunkenness, one committed suicide, and one went insane. The *Somers* herself, four years later, capsized off Vera Cruz, Mexico, and drowned 40 of her crew.

"Mark of the beast" is a nickname for the white patch on the lapels of a British midshipman's uniform.

"No quarter," meaning a determination to fight to the death, takes it meaning from the reverse of "giving quarter," an old custom by which officers, upon surrender, could ransom themselves by paying "one quarter of their year's pay."

Keel haul • In the old days keel-hauling was a brutal punishment inflicted on seamen guilty of mutiny or some other high crime. It practically amounted to a death sentence, for the chances of recovery after the ordeal were slight.

The culprit was fastened to a line which had been passed beneath the vessel's keel. He was then dragged under the water on the starboard side of the ship, hauled along the barnacle-encrusted bottom and hoisted up and onto the deck on the port side.

If the barnacles didn't cut him to pieces, and if he didn't drown, he was considered to have paid for his crime and was free, but his chances were mighty slim.

Chipping with a rubber hammer. An old-time superstition regarding eternal punishment for wicked seamen, pictured them forever hopelessly chipping . . . with a hammer made of rubber.

Get the point? When a British officer is court-martialed, the verdict of the court is made plain to him by placing his sword on a table. If the hilt is toward him, he has been found not guilty; if the point is toward him, he has been found guilty; he "gets the point" without a word being said.

Posted at Lloyds • When a ship is wrecked, sinks, or just plain disappears, the fact is stated on a bulletin board at Lloyds, the famous marine insurance company in London. (*See also* A-1 at Lloyds.)

Crossing the line • When a ship crosses the Equator, all those aboard who are doing so for the first time, known as "Pollywogs," are initiated into the "Ancient Order of the Deep" by those who have crossed before, the "Shellbacks." This ceremony had its origin in antiquity; long ago such initiations were held when ships sailed south across the 30th parallel of latitude, or when they passed through the Straits of Gibraltar. The ceremony probably originated with the Vikings, who passed it on to the Angles, Saxons, and Normans.

In the U.S. Navy, men who cross the line are given an elaborate certificate attesting to the fact, as well as a small card for their billfold or card case. Probably the biggest mass initiation of pollywogs in the U.S. Navy took place in 1935, when the entire Pacific Fleet steamed south from Panama just far enough to cross the line. A crossing-the-line party can be very elaborate, with men costumed as King Neptune, Davey Jones, Queen Amphritite, the Royal Baby, Royal Bears, Royal Cops, Royal Barber, Royal Chaplain, Royal Navigator, and any number of other characters. When a ship crosses the line, rank has no privilege—a senior officer who is still a pollywog is initiated along with all the lesser fry.

Paddy's Milestone • The island Ailsa Craig, near the entrance to Glasgow harbor, became known as Paddy's Milestone because of the large number of Irishmen who crossed to Scotland. They gave it the affectionate nickname because they were cheered by the nearness of their goal when they sighted the island.

"*Boondocks*" is a slang term for any remote out-of-the-way place. The term supposedly came from the Philippine village of Bondoc, across the bay from Manila. Heavy boots are called boondockers.

"*Pollywog*" is any sailor who has not crossed the Equator. Those who have are Shellbacks.

Dead Horse • In the early days, both in Merchant Marine and Navy, men were allowed to draw advance pay when going on a long cruise. Such a payment was called a dead horse, possibly because the money was spent before it was earned and a man was in the position of having to work the first few months without earning any more money—he might as well have spent his money for a dead horse. It used to be customary, after men had worked out their advance on wages, to hold a ceremony in which a rude horse made out of a barrel and odds and ends of boards and canvas was thrown overboard and set afire, while the men sang a chantey called "Poor old horse." In the Navy, even yet, an advance on pay when being transferred is called a dead horse.

Pay on the cap. A tradition in the British Navy is that enlisted men receive their pay on their cap tops. This was originally done so that all could see the amount paid and any errors could be corrected.

Horse latitudes were, roughly speaking, the Atlantic ocean between latitudes thirty and forty degrees north. The term was coined in the days when sailing ships carrying horses from Europe to America were often becalmed there. As food and water ran low, some of the horses, who had no vote in the matter, would be thrown overboard in an effort to save the rest of them.

Camel cargo. In 1856 the United States sent the USS *Supply* to Smyrna to bring back a load of 50 camels, which it was believed could replace Army mules in the southwest. The camels were unloaded in Powder Horn, Texas, on 13 May 1856. Soldiers used to mules didn't care for camels, and the camels didn't much care for Texas. Sold out of the Army, a few of them went to a circus and the rest were turned loose in Arizona. A few survived until about 1905.

Quaker guns were carried by many ships in the 17th century. They were wooden guns, closely resembling the real thing, added to the battery to create an impression of being heavily armed and to discourage pirates.

Columbia, a three-master out of Boston, was the first American ship to sail around the world. She made the trip in one month less than three years from 1787 to 1790. The Columbia River in Oregon is now named for the ship, but before she arrived there it was called the Oregon River.

"Cape Cod turkey," in the old sailing ship days, referred to salted codfish.

Bamboozle is a perfectly good dictionary word which had its origin in an early day colloquialism. It meant the act of deceiving passing vessels as to your nationality, by flying some ensign other than your own; a common practice of pirates.

Sword-hilt cross • In medieval days every Christian knight had a cross embossed on the hilt of his sword as a solemn token that he would keep the faith. To this day, the dirk worn by British midshipmen carries on its hilt the emblem of religious fealty.

Scurvy trick • This commonly used phrase had a distinctly nautical origin.

In the old days of sail and interminable voyages, lack of fresh vegetables and clean drinking water made scurvy one of the most dreaded diseases which beset the deepwatermen. It was a loathsome plague, so scurvy is certainly apt, when the phrase is used to describe a particularly dirty deal.

Three-mile limit is, by international law, the distance over which a nation has jurisdiction of its coastal waters. At the time that limit was established, three miles was the longest range of any guns; beyond that no nation could enforce its laws. The old three-mile limit has been replaced, in some instances, by a twelve-mile limit; some nations now enforce a 200-mile limit to prevent fishing in their waters.

Miniature salute • The U.S. Naval Academy owns a model of the French three-decker *Ville de Paris* with a very historic and unique background. At Dresden in 1814, Alexander the First of Russia was given a 120-gun salute from the little brass cannon peeping from the model's gunports.

Fleet, a group of ships operating together, comes from the Anglo-Saxon *floet.*

Women at sea • The British Navy used to permit women on board its ships during long cruises; a woman named Ann Johnson actually served as a member of a gun crew and was killed during the Battle of Copenhagen (2 April 1801). American clipper ship captains used to carry their wives on board. The hospital at the Merchant Marine Academy at Kings Point, New York, is named for the wife of a clipper skipper. She was Mary Patten, 19 years old; when her husband became ill on a trip from the East Coast in 1856 she took command, navigated the ship around the Horn and into San Francisco in a 120-day trip. During World War II many women served aboard merchant ships.

Naval War College. All navies have such an institution, of one sort or another, in which officers receive advanced training. The first war college of record was established at Sagres, Portugal, in 1415, by Prince Henry, the Navigator. The U.S. Naval War College was established at Newport, Rhode Island, on 6 October 1884. The first superintendent there was Commander Stephen B. Luce.

Practice makes perfect • The aircraft carrier *Lexington,* operating as a training ship in the Gulf of Mexico, counted 350,000 arrested landings between 1955 and 1975.

"When my ship comes in," meaning "When I make my fortune" comes from the days when merchants sent ships out in search of rich cargoes. To finance such a venture, they borrowed from money-lenders. As it was impossible to set an exact date when they would repay the loan, they would sign documents promising to pay "when my ship comes in." Shakespeare refers to this in *The Merchant of Venice:* "... three of your argosies are richly come to harbour suddenly."

Tons of Treasure • One of the first ships to reach America, the *Golden Hind* under Sir Francis Drake, touched north of San Francisco about 1578–79; then returned to England with a load of gold and silver looted from the Spanish. At present value, her cargo would be worth about $50,000,000. Drake didn't get all of the treasure. In February, 1942, the submarine *Trout* off-loaded ammunition at Corregidor, and needed ballast. No sand bags could be spared, so she was given 20 tons of gold and silver instead, to deliver to U.S. authorities in Hawaii. In 1944 the Liberty Ship *John Barry* sailed for Russia with silver bullion worth $26,000,000 in her cargo. A German submarine torpedoed her in the Arabian Sea and the silver is still there—2 miles down.

Listless, meaning dull or lifeless, was coined in the days of sail when a ship was becalmed and rode on an even keel, without the usual port or starboard list experienced under a good breeze. No wind, no list; listless, no pep.

"Above board," a slang term for honesty, originated in the days when pirates would hide most of their crews behind the bulwarks in order to lure some unsuspecting victim into thinking they were honest merchantmen. It followed that anyone who displayed all his crew openly on deck was obviously an honest seaman.

At Logger-heads • This term, descriptive of the angry relationship between two parties, dates back to the days when tools called logger-heads were used in spreading hot pitch along deck seams. The tool consisted of a wooden pole with an iron head something like a flattened adze.

Men doing this work for long hours were apt to grow nerve-raw and quarrelsome, and their logger-heads made effective and ugly weapons. A fight with these tools was a deadly knock-'em-down-and-drag-'em-out foray, and the seriousness of the affair is the general inference in the phrase "they are at logger-heads."

Red bulwarks • In the 18th century, the gun decks and bulwarks of fighting ships were painted red. This was done so that men would not be dismayed by the sight of blood splattered around during battle.

Round-the-world-cruises • The first ship to actually sail all the way around the world was the Spanish *Victoria,* with Sebastian del Cano as captain—the only one of five that sailed from San Lucar, Spain, on 20 September 1519, ever to return. She came home on 6 September 1522.

The first American merchant ship to sail around the world was the *Columbia,* of Boston. She departed on 30 September 1787 and returned in August 1790. The first naval vessel to circumnavigate the globe was the USS *Vincennes,* which left New York on 31 August 1826 and returned on 8 June 1830. In 1838 the Wilkes Expedition of six ships sailed from New York on a trip that covered over 85,000 miles. Only the flagship, *Vincennes,* completed the trip, returning in June 1842. The next round-the-world trip by a group of vessels was made by the "White Fleet" of 16 battleships and auxiliaries; they sailed from Hampton Roads, Virginia, on 16 December 1907 and returned on 22 February 1909.

In 1960 the submarine *Triton* made a trip entirely around the world, submerged, following in general the path of Magellan's ships. She completed the trip in 84 days. The first steam-powered ship of the Navy to circumnavigate the globe was the *Ticonderoga,* which made the trip from Hampton Roads between 7 December 1878 and 9 November 1880.

The first group of ships ever to sail entirely around the world without refueling included the carrier *Enterprise,* guided-missile cruiser *Long Beach,* and frigate *Bainbridge,* all nuclear-powered, which made the 30,560-mile eastbound trip in 64 days.

Tourists began making round-the-world trips in the 1890s, but they sailed in more than one ship, breaking the cruise by taking a train across the United States from the Pacific to the Atlantic. In 1922 the Cunard liner *Laconia* made the first round-the-world trip in which passengers rode the same ship all the way.

Flying Dutchman. The legendary Dutch captain, Van der Decken, trying to take his ship *Flying Dutchman* around the Cape of Good Hope, cursed the stormy ocean and was, in punishment for his blasphemy, sentenced to sail his ship there for ever after. Superstitious sailors still see the ship there in stormy weather. In July 1881, as HMS *Bacchante* cruised off the Cape, a lookout reported seeing the *Flying Dutchman*; King George V, who was aboard, described it in his diary. The lookout who sighted the ship fell from a mast and was killed a few hours later. The *Flying Dutchman* was seen as recently as October 1959, when the Dutch freighter *Straat Magelhaen* reported having met her off the Cape. In 1843 the German composer, Richard Wagner, completed an opera titled *Der Fliegende Hollander,* or *The Flying Dutchman,* based on the legend.

Megaphone, that invaluable aid to OODs and girl cheerleaders alike, is no new invention. Alexander the Great used one in 335 BC.

"Hugh Williams" might be almost anyone, but in British slang it refers to a sole survivor of a sea tragedy. The term is based on the odd fact that, over some two hundred years, nearly forty sole survivors of shipwrecks and ship sinkings were named Hugh Williams.

People by the shipload • During the Allied evacuation at Hungnam, Korea, in 1950, the SS *Meredith Victory* set an all time record for passenger carrying. She was a cargo ship, not designed to carry passengers at all, but she loaded out more than 14,000 Korean refugees for the trip to Pusan.

The record didn't last long. As U.S. forces began the evacuation of Saigon in the spring of 1975, some 179,000 Vietnamese refugees were hauled out by ships of the Military Sealift Command. In one trip, from Danang to Phu Quoc Island in the Gulf of Siam, the SS *Pioneer Contender* loaded 16,600 refugees.

Bottle message. In old sea tales, shipwrecked sailors scribbled a message, stuffed it in a bottle and tossed it into the sea, hoping someone would find it and learn what happened to them. For many years the U.S. Navy furnished "bottle papers" to mariners who dropped them overboard with notations as to when and where they were "launched." People who found these papers returned them to the Navy, and in this way ocean currents were charted.

The longest trip made by a bottle paper began when it was dropped overboard from the SS *Linfield Victory* off Japan on 6 March 1948. It finally turned up on the beach at Reedsport, Oregon, twenty-seven years later.

The shortest bottle-trip on record was made by one thrown overboard from the destroyer *Jouett* in Lahaina Roads, Hawaii, in 1940. The bottle was spotted by another ship at Lahaina and was returned to the *Jouett* the very next day.

Coast Guard • The United States Coast Guard was formed in 1915 by a combination of the Revenue Cutter Service and the Lifesaving Service. The motto of the Coast Guard Service is *Semper Paratus,* "Always Ready."

The history of the Coast Guard goes back to 1790 when the Revenue Service was created by the Secretary of the Treasury, Alexander Hamilton. The first vessels were ten cutters, ranging from 30 to 50 tons in size.

Arrive, meaning to reach one's destination, was once a purely nautical expression. It comes from the Latin *arripare*—to come to land.

"Yankee," a nickname for Americans, was first applied only to people from New England, and during the Civil War, only to Northerners. The name originated in colonial times, when Dutch settlers in New York referred to those from Connecticut as *Jan Kees,* meaning "John Cheese."

Cheese-paring. This much-used term has lost entirely its original meaning. Today, cheese-paring describes the niggardly person who squeezes each nickel 'till it's thin as a dime.

Originally, cheese-paring was petty theft. Shipmasters carrying cargoes of cheese from Holland to London would steal the mould-ridge from the balls of cheese, and press them into extra balls for their own profits.

As they used knives in the whittling-down process, they became known as "cheese-parers," or in less polite language cheats or thieves.

Cheesebox on a Raft! That was the derisive term applied to the USS *Monitor,* the Civil War ironclad with a revolving turret that fought the Confederate ironclad *Virginia* in the famous Battle of Hampton Roads on 9 March 1862. The *Monitor-Virginia* battle doomed all wooden ships; after that, the navies of the world built steam-powered, iron-hulled ships. The *Monitor* sank off Cape Hatteras in a storm the night of 31 December 1862, and for over a hundred years her exact location was a mystery. Finally, in 1973, she was discovered through the endeavors of mid-shipmen at the U.S. Naval Academy. The area of the ocean bottom where the *Monitor* lies has been declared the first Marine Sanctuary in the United States.

"Hungry Hundred," back in the gay nineties, was a nickname for the first Royal Navy Reserve officers assigned to duty with the fleet; it referred to the fact that there were not many of them, and that their pay was very low.

Bootlegger, meaning one who conducts an illegal trade in liquor, was first used during the reign of King George III, to describe smugglers who hid valuables in their huge sea-boots when dodging His Majesty's coastguardsmen.

Buccaneers were pirates and sea rovers from England, France and the Netherlands who roamed the Caribbean in the 17th century. The term comes from the French *boucanier,* which comes from a Caribe word *boucan* which meant "dried meat." The pirates learned how to prepare the meat, carried on an illegal trade in it—with piracy as a sideline—and so acquired a name which meant only that they were expert beef-smokers.

"Close quarters," a term now used to express hard fighting, was originally "closed quarters" and referred specifically to special deck-houses where the crew could take refuge if boarders tried to take the ship. The doors were barred and loopholed, so a deadly fire could be poured into the enemy.

War at sea has been going on for a long time. The earliest recorded naval battle took place in 480 BC off the Greek port of Salamis, near the present city of Athens. A Persian invasion force of 600 ships was defeated by a Greek fleet only half as large.

Slipped his cable. A sailor who dies is said to have "slipped his cable." The term comes from the fact that only in great emergency, such as escaping an enemy in a hurry, does a vessel willingly leave cable and anchor on the sea-floor when she departs her anchorage. Even more to the point, she never expects to return to that port.

Brick Battleship • The USS *Illinois,* a ship that never went to sea or even served in the Navy, was visited by more people than ever went aboard all other ships in the Navy at that time. She was an exact replica of an *Oregon*-class battleship, built on a platform resting on pilings in Lake Michigan, for the Chicago World's Fair in 1893. The ship was built of bricks covered with cement, but many of the more than 3,000,000 people who went aboard her were certain they had been aboard an actual battleship.

"Gone west," an expression referring to men killed in action, dates back to an ancient Viking custom of burial. When a Viking chief died, his body was placed aboard his ship, or galley. Then, the sail was set, the steering oar lashed to keep her on course, and she was set afire and pushed off to sail westward. The expression, *"knocked galley west,"* meaning someone was knocked cold or stiff, is derived from the same custom.

Viking is pronounced *veek-ing,* and refers to those wild sea robbers who laid in wait for their victims in the *veeks* or bays in Norway.

Coins for Charon ● The custom of placing coins under the step of a mast when a ship is building had its origin with the ancient Romans. It was a custom then to place coins in the mouth of a dead person in the belief this would enable him to pay Charon to ferry him across the river Styx. This custom has continued ever since; a Spanish wreck found off England had a coin dated 1618 under its mast. When the USS *New Orleans* was built (she was launched in 1933) officers placed a total of 33 coins under her foremast and mainmast. The coins were pennies, nickels and dimes, all "heads up."

Galley west, as used in the expression "knocked him galley west" is a reminder that the Vikings, when a chief died, placed his body aboard his galley or long boat, and after setting it afire, started it sailing toward the west. The old British term was *collywest.*

78

Bibliography

Almanac of Naval Facts ed. by Arnold S. Lott. Annapolis: U.S. Naval Institute, 1964.

American Voyages to the Orient Charles Oscar Paullin. Annapolis: U.S. Naval Institute, 1971.

America's Maritime Heritage Eloise Engle and Arnold S. Lott. Annapolis: U.S. Naval Institute Press, 1975.

An Encyclopedia of World History William L. Langer. Boston: Houghton Mifflin Company, 1960.

Bluejackets' Manual ed. by Arnold S. Lott. Annapolis: U.S. Naval Institute Press, 1973.

Brewer's Dictionary of Phrase & Fable rev. Ivor H. Evans. New York: Harper & Row, 1970.

California Gold Rush New York: American Heritage Publishing Co., 1961.

Dictionary of Military and Naval Quotations Robert Debs Heinl. Annapolis: U.S. Naval Institute, 1966.

Dictionary of Modern English Usage London: Oxford University Press, 1965.

Gold of Ophir Sydney Greenbie and Marjorie Greenbie. Garden City: Doubleday, Page & Co., 1925.

Greyhounds of the Sea Carl C. Cutler. Annapolis: U.S. Naval Institute, 1967.

History of Marine Navigation W. E. May. New York: W. W. Norton & Co., Inc., 1973.

Junks and Sampans of the Yangtse River C. R. G. Worcester. Annapolis: U.S. Naval Institute, 1971.

Naval Customs and Traditions Leland P. Lovette. Annapolis: U.S. Naval Institute, 1939.

Romance of Navigation W. B. Whall. New York: Robert M. McBride & Co., 1926.

Sailing and Small Craft Down the Ages Edgar L. Bloomster. Annapolis: U.S. Naval Institute, 1940.

Sea and Man Jorma Pohjanpalo. New York: Stein and Day, 1970.

Ships and Sailors William H. Clark. Boston: L. C. Page & Co., 1938.

Skylab, Our First Space Station NASA SP 238. Washington, D.C., GPO, 1977.

Supership Noel Mostert. New York: Alfred A. Knopf, 1974.

Uniforms of the Sea Services Robert H. Rankin. Annapolis: U.S. Naval Institute, 1962.